IN MY FATHER'S BAKERY

A BRONX MEMOIR

IN MY FATHER'S BAKERY
A BRONX MEMOIR

MARVIN KORMAN

Red Rock Press   New York, New York

Cover painting by Abe Echevarria

Book design by Paul Perlow

Red Rock Press
Suite 114
459 Columbus Avenue
New York, New York 10024

www.RedRockPress.com

Korman, Marvin 1927-
In My Father's Bakery: A Bronx Memoir
    p. cm
ISBN: 0-9714372-4-6
Jews—New York (State)—New York—Social Life and customs—20th
Century—Anecdotes. 2. Jews—New York (State)— New York—Biography. 3.
Bronx (New York, N.Y.)—Social Life and customs—20th
Century—Anecdotes. 4. Bronx (New York, N.Y.)—Biography. 5. Korman,
Marvin, 1927—Childhood and youth. 1. Title.
  F128.9.J5K67 2003
  974.7'275004924-dc21

                            2003005201

ACKNOWLEDGMENTS

Writing is generally a solitary endeavor. However, the act of turning a piece of writing into a book for publication is anything but. I am fortunate that there were many people I could count on to help me in the transformation.

So, when I call your names, please step forward and take a bow: Dale Burg, Father Joseph Cogo of Our Lady of Pompeii Church in Greenwich Village, Gladys Chen, Flora Marshall Gayuski, Nat Gold, Bill Henick, Grace Lee, Bob Kavesh, Jess Korman, Jane Pasanen, Evelynne Patterson, Judy Paul, Irwin Z. Robinson, Laura Tosi of the Bronx County Historical Society and Ed Wallace.

And my agent, Julia Lord, who is both smart and determined, and my editor, Ilene Barth, who is also smart and determined, and who showed me how to bring form and unity to what was often a series of disparate and jumbled remembrances. And to Sylvia Baumgarten, my copyeditor, who is both relentless and forgiving.

A special thanks goes to my daughter Candy Korman, who was one of my first readers and my most consistent cheerleader.

And, finally, to my wife, Eleanore, who has given more thoughtful suggestions to this project than anyone would think possible, and who has endured some pretty strange and cantankerous behavior from me during this past year.

*This book is dedicated to
Eleanore Zolotow Korman,
the best thing that ever
happened to me.*

INTRODUCTION

My father's bakery was my first university. As a schoolboy I did my homework there, sitting at one of the small wooden tables in the rear of the shop. It was easy to eavesdrop on the conversations of my father and his cronies or the neighborhood merchants who would stop in for coffee and a Danish, or to listen to the lighthearted banter between the saleswomen behind the counters and their customers, who would purchase a few Kaiser rolls or perhaps a bread—and just maybe an apple crumb cake or a couple of éclairs.

There was nothing automatic about buying dessert. It was during the Great Depression, and most of these women had to think twice about spending that extra fifty cents from the family food budget. But while they were thinking, they talked, and often it was about a great deal more than cake.

At one time or another, just about everyone in our Bronx neighborhood (known as the Tremont section) stopped into Grossfeld & Korman's Bakery, which was at 935 East 180th Street—three blocks from the Bronx Zoo.

My grandfather, Herschel Grossfeld, and his son-in-law, my father, Nathan Korman, opened this bakery in 1920. My father had learned his craft working in my grandfather's bakery in Yorkville, the old German neighborhood in Manhattan. They reasoned, I suppose, that the then suburban Bronx offered new opportunities for business, and was a fine place, not only for my mother, Lillian, and my father to raise a family, but for my aunts and uncles as well.

My sister, Edith, was born in 1921; I arrived in 1927. My mother, along with her sisters, all worked in the bakery as salesclerks, bringing their offspring into the shop where they could keep an eye on them—which is why I grew up among pumpernickels, strawberry shortcakes and apple pies, listening to the grown-ups talk.

Maybe three quarters of the people who populated the apartment buildings in the bakery's immediate neighborhood were Jewish. The rest were Hungarian, Czech and Polish Catholics who, like the Jews, had prospered sufficiently to leave the tenement neighborhoods that had first received them or their forebears. There were a few descendants of the Dutch, English and German settlers who had arrived when grass and not cement grew in the Bronx. The Irish lived at the southern edge of the neighborhood, while Italians clustered to the northwest around Arthur Avenue, which still boasts several great Italian restaurants and food shops. African-Americans, or "Coloreds" or Negroes as they were called then, were almost as rare as Russian nobility, and only a few ventured into the Tremont section, mainly to work.

Remarkably, everyone seemed to get along with one another, for the most part. During the Great Depression, the shop owners along 180th Street—my father among them—were relatively well off compared to the rest of the neighborhood. Still, there was the overall feeling of "we're all in this together." This positive attitude was intensified after Pearl Harbor.

The only blight on neighborhood harmony, as far I was concerned, came from some of the Irish kids from the St. Thomas Aquinas Church and School on Daly Avenue. The Irish boys liked to pick on the smaller kids, whom they assumed to be Jewish; occasionally I heard the taunt "Christ-killers" roll off their lips. Some of them earned pocket money selling copies of Father Coughlin's *Social Justice*, the weekly that quoted from the *Protocols of the Elders of Zion* and heaped praise on Adolf Hitler.

There were some modest fistfights, generally initiated by the Irish kids, but the Jews gave as good at they got. And, as a kind of counterbalance, there were stickball games that were played between the two rival religious groups without any apparent difficulties. These took place on Southern Boulevard, near the trolley car barns, where the adults sat on stone benches and cheered the participants.

By the time I was ten, I had less time for street games because—in addition to doing my homework in my father's bakery—I was working there, folding the thin cardboard boxes that were used to package the cakes and cookies sold by my mother and aunts. My older sister and cousins worked there as well. As the youngest of the lot, I was happy to be included. My tasks grew as I grew. My favorite, at the beginning, was squeezing the jelly into the jelly donuts. The conversational buzz—in dazzling combinations of Polish, Russian, Yiddish, Hungarian and English—never ceased.

My father's bakery was the center of my growing-up years, but my life didn't stop there. So, included here are stories that began in the bakery but continued elsewhere—at my parents' or other relatives' homes or on excursions I made from the bakery, almost always in the company of my father or another adult who worked there. A few remembrances start in another place entirely, or continue through decades, but, as you will see, they are all connected, like an umbilical cord, to the bakery.

What I learned during my young years, observing and listening to the diverse voices of the world of my father's bakery, has colored every aspect of my life and, I would like to think, enriched it. And while that place and time has all but vanished, its aromas still linger in my imagination.

If I have erred in this memoir in recording a name or fact, or have recollected an incident differently than another participant might have, I hope you will understand. After all, I'm seeing this through the prism of many years, and sometimes the eye (and the brain) can get a little blurry, as if a handful of flour had been tossed in its way.

Here, then, is some of what I breathed in, some of what I saw and some of what I heard.

—Marvin Korman
2003

TABLE OF CONTENTS

Uncle Maxie Strikes Back

The Irish didn't like it
when they heard of Greenberg's fame
for they thought a good first baseman
should possess an Irish name.
—Edgar A. Guest

My Uncle Maxie was born on New Year's Day 1900 in the Yorkville section of Manhattan. He was the male half of the second set of twins produced by my maternal grandparents. His birth, along with that of his sister, my Aunt Bertha, was cause for great celebration in the household, which then boasted six children. Two more would come before my grandmother said, "Enough is enough."

Uncle Maxie was considered a delightful child, and was just beginning to enjoy the sports and social activities that ten-year-olds engaged in—swimming off the docks along the East River and running through the wooded areas of Central Park right behind the Metropolitan Museum of Art—when he was struck with what was either rheumatic fever or scarlet fever. I was never sure which. In any case, according to my mother who was four years Maxie's senior, he was never quite the same after he recovered. He became withdrawn and frightened of being around people, except his immediate family. Both his athletic and intellectual skills never developed beyond the time he became ill.

Naturally, school became an enormous problem for him and, as soon as he finished seventh grade—several years older than his classmates—he was put to work in the family bakery on 82nd Street and First Avenue. Rather than work as a baker, which would have required a great deal of strength and stamina, he became a salesclerk, a job that was usually assigned to the women in the family.

From the beginning, my father's bakery was as much a haven for Uncle Maxie as it would later become for me; I would go there after school to sit at one of the old tables in the rear of the store, next to the glistening brass coffee urns, and try to do my homework. Long after the ovens in the cellar had been left to cool for the day and the last of the breads and cakes had been hoisted up on the large wooden dumbwaiter to the street-level shop, the aromas of freshly baked ryes and pumpernickels would mingle with sweet smells of fruit pies, chocolate cakes and pastries.

The store was much longer than it was wide, with sales counters and display cases on only one side. Along the opposite wall was a series of wooden tables, where simple breakfasts and lunches were served. In the rear of the shop, separated by a swinging door from the eating and selling areas were both my father's office and a simple kitchen.

From my vantage point, I would look up occasionally and observe the customers, mainly women, as they surveyed the display of breads and cakes and chatted with the salesclerks. There were two sales counters, one for selling breads and one for selling cakes. The bread counter was simply a long wooden board on which were placed two or three metal baskets piled high with rolls and breads. The cake counter was more elaborate and was shielded from the customers by glass. Several shelves held trays of cookies, French and Danish pastries, and other small cakes laid out in even rows. Separating the two counters was a large, ornate cash register.

Uncle Maxie worked the bread counter. The other salesclerks moved effortlessly between the counters. But Uncle Maxie could not handle the variety of items offered at the cake counter; if a customer indicated that she wanted cake as well as bread, Maxie would simply ask her to go to another clerk.

The steady customers knew this about Uncle Maxie and they accepted whatever inconvenience his limitations might have caused them. In fact, many of them preferred to have Uncle Maxie serve them, even if it was only for breads and rolls, because his ever-present smile seemed to indicate the sheer delight he took in serving them. He projected a gentle warmth with every loaf of rye he sold.

In addition to only working the bread counter, Uncle Maxie stayed home on Fridays, Saturdays and Sundays, the busiest days for the bakery. Crowds, noise, rapid movements and anything that was not part of his usual routine made him extremely nervous. The family did everything it could to protect him.

My cousin Jerry and I were the happy beneficiaries of Uncle Maxie's limitations. Every Sunday, from April through September, when the New York Giants baseball team was playing at the Polo Grounds, Uncle Maxie took us to the game. We never went to Yankee Stadium, because Uncle Maxie was a Giants fan, the result of his Manhattan youth.

The Polo Grounds was located on the Manhattan side of the Bronx River at 155th Street. Yankee Stadium was and still is located at 161st Street in the Bronx. This seemingly minor geographical distinction was further exacerbated by the fact that Uncle Maxie had grown up hating the Yankees. As a result, without much prodding, my cousin Jerry and I became diehard Giant fans. Our heroes were Mel Ott, Bill Terry and the lefty/righty pitching sensations, King Carl (Hubbell) and Prince Hal (Schumacher).

But, beginning in 1934 and reaching its climax in 1938, almost every Jewish Bronxite—male and female, young and old—claimed dual citizenship with the city of Detroit. This was true for Yankee fans and Giant fans alike. The reason was a charming, self-effacing young man named Hank Greenberg, the son of Jewish-Rumanian immigrants, who was playing first base for the Detroit Tigers.

Many people have questioned why the Yankees had not pursued the East Bronx native and star athlete at James Monroe High School. Actually, the Yankees did try to sign Greenberg but he wasn't stupid. The Yankees already had the "Iron Man," Lou Gehrig, at first base, and even "Hammerin' Hank" figured that there was little chance of anyone replacing Gehrig in the near future.

So Greenberg signed with the Detroit organization and quickly established himself as a star player, helping the Tigers win the American League Championship in 1934 and a World Series in 1935, the same year in which he was voted the League's Most Valuable Player. There had been Jewish major league ball players before Greenberg, but none had been so dominant in the game.

Greenberg's prowess on the field was one thing, but what endeared him to Jewish families in the Bronx, and presumably elsewhere, was his decision in 1934 not to play on Yom Kippur, the Day of Atonement and the holiest day of the year for Jews, even though the game was important to Detroit's chances of winning the pennant.

Talk about Hank Greenberg permeated every area of life in the Bronx. Even my grandfather—for whom the word "game" meant pinochle or hearts, and for whom "balls and strikes" meant dancing parties and picket lines—would question me as we folded cake boxes at the back table of the bakery: "So, you think Hank will hit a home run today?"

My grandfather's brother, Menashe, who reigned over the bread and roll production in the bakery and who rarely left the scorching heat of the ovens during a twelve-hour day, also showed curiosity. What did it mean, he asked me, when they said Hank Greenberg played "first base?" Was that good? he wondered.

In 1938, Greenberg began to hit home runs at a rate that would give him—by the end of the season—more than the record of 60 set by Babe Ruth in 1927. My cousin and I made subtle suggestions to

Uncle Maxie that we would love to see Greenberg in action when the Tigers came to the Bronx to play the Yankees. Maybe we were too subtle, because he acted as if he hadn't heard us.

But one Tuesday morning in August, something happened that changed everything. Uncle Maxie was, as usual, behind the bread counter. A woman came into the bakery and asked him for six nicely browned Kaiser rolls and a rye bread with lots of caraway seeds.

Uncle Maxie, who could remember for years exactly what breads a customer had asked for, smiled as he carefully selected the rolls and bread and tenderly placed them in a paper bag.

Uncle Maxie politely asked the new customer for twenty-seven cents.

At this point, the woman asked for some apple cake and a marble loaf.

"You can get them at the cake counter," my uncle replied, as he always did when a customer's order went beyond bread. "One of the girls will . . . "

The woman objected loudly. "Why do I have to go to two clerks?"

Uncle Maxie stammered: "I . . . I don't do cakes."

"Whatta you mean, 'You don't do cakes?' What are you—some kinda dummy?" the woman screamed.

Uncle Maxie froze, and then he began to shake. My mother, who had been waiting on a customer at the cake counter, rushed to her younger brother. She put her arms around him and tried to comfort him. By then, he was crying uncontrollably.

"Now see what you've done," my mother shouted at the woman.

"What *I've* done? I didn't do nothing!"

"You called him a dummy."

"Are you people crazy?" the woman said as she reached into her pocketbook. "Here's your lousy twenty-seven cents. I'll buy my cake elsewhere." She stormed out of the store.

My father, who was getting ready for his "Tuesday afternoon off," told my mother he would walk Uncle Maxie home to his apartment on Bronx Park South, a few blocks from the store. Uncle Maxie lived there with my grandfather.

"Look, Maxie, it was nothing. Just a stupid woman," my father said.

"I tried to tell her to let one of the girls get her some cake . . . "

"I know, but it's best that you take the rest of the day off. I would take you to the track with me but I know you hate the horses."

"Yeah. I hate the horses."

"You should take tomorrow off, too."

"Okay."

"Hey, the Tigers are in town. Tomorrow, why don't you take the boys to Yankee Stadium? They're dying to see Hank Greenberg."

"I don't go to the Stadium. I hate the Yankees."

"That's just it. You can go there and root *against* them."

Uncle Maxie smiled.

"Good," my father said. He reached into his wallet and handed Uncle Maxie a ten-dollar bill. "Get some really good seats. You know, field level."

"They cost two-twenty each," Uncle Maxie said.

"That's okay. You can buy 'em some sodas and peanuts, too."

The following afternoon, my Aunt Bertha, Jerry's mother, made chicken salad sandwiches which Jerry and I devoured in the rear of the bakery. We finished off our lunch with chocolate brownies and milk. Life was good. And the prospect of seeing our hero, Hank Greenberg, only added to our joy.

"Do you think he'll hit a homer today?" I asked.

"Of course he will," Jerry replied. Jerry was three years older than I, so I knew he was right.

Uncle Maxie came by the bakery at one o'clock and we walked to the elevated trains at Boston Road; we took one to 149th Street, where we changed for a different line and took the train uptown for two stops, and getting off at the unfamiliar 161st Street station.

I had to admit that Yankee Stadium was very impressive. It looked much larger than the home of our beloved Giants.

"Stay close to me," Uncle Maxie said. "I gotta find the ticket booths. I don't like this place."

Jerry and I knew there was really nothing wrong with Yankee Stadium; it was just Uncle Maxie being Uncle Maxie.

A few minutes later we found a series of ticket windows and Uncle Maxie got on one of the lines. People were milling about, and I noticed that many of them carried orange and black pennants with the words "Detroit Tigers." I figured that if the banners said "Hank Greenberg" they might have sold even more.

Our seats were field level behind the Yankees' dugout. That way we could look across to the visitor's dugout and watch Hank Greenberg as he waited for his turn to bat. Also, we could see him up close as he fielded his position at first base. Uncle Maxie tipped the usher a quarter and the man used an oversized chamois cloth glove to wipe off our seats.

It took us a few minutes to adjust our eyes to the dimensions of the stadium and the vastly superior location of our seats. Seeing a game from box seats—practically on the field—was a great deal different than seeing it from the upper deck of the Polo Grounds. The players looked huge.

At about a quarter to two, the Tigers began their batting practice. Everyone had been anticipating the appearance of Greenberg, and when he left the dugout, there was a burst of applause and a thunderous roar from the crowd, many of whom were still making their way to their seats. He trotted over to the batting cage and stood quietly, waiting his turn. All eyes were on the greatest ball player the Bronx had ever produced: our very own hometown hero. Jerry and I stood up, cheering wildly. Uncle Maxie remained seated but I saw him smile ever so slightly.

Greenberg stepped into the batter's box, took a couple of practice swings and then pounded the first pitch about 400 feet into the centerfield bleachers. He drove the next two pitches like bullets into the gap between left and center fields. It was: Boom! Boom! Boom! Hank was looking good. I hoped he wouldn't leave it all on the practice field.

As the game was about to start, at precisely 3:05, we became aware of a loud voice that was coming from a heavyset, brutish-looking guy seated about six rows behind us, drinking beer at a furious rate.

"Hey, Greenberg, did ya momma feed ya matzo balls? . . . ya swing like a fuckin' pansy . . . you better watch ya head, today . . . go back to Russia, Jew-boy."

A few people in the seats around us tried to respond, and I saw one of them talk to the usher, who shrugged his shoulders and walked away.

Frankly, I was accustomed to hearing talk like that, which was usually directed at my friends and me when we were playing near the St. Thomas Aquinas parochial school on Daly Avenue. But since my mother only made matzo balls for the Passover seder, and I didn't know what a pansy was, and my family was German not Russian, that kind of talk never bothered me much. But I was worried about Uncle Maxie. He'd had a fit when the woman had called him a dummy the day before, so I watched him very closely.

The first inning began in a most extraordinary way. The Yankee pitcher walked the first three Detroit batters, loading the bases for Hank Greenberg. He lumbered to the plate. His massive six-foot-four-inch body sloped slightly as his feet dug into the batter's box. I realized that he had within his power the opportunity to beat the New York Yankees in their own ballpark, to move one home run closer to Babe Ruth's record, and to bring undreamed happiness to thousands of Jewish youths from the Grand Concourse to Westchester Avenue. And, most important, he could shut the mouth of the guy sitting six rows behind us.

Greenberg teased the thousands of fans by stepping out of the batter's box after each pitch was thrown. The tension grew and the fans leaned forward in their seats. When the count reached one ball and two strikes, the Yankee pitcher launched a high, inside fastball—obviously a mistake—that Greenberg drove over the head of the Yankee left fielder, Myril Hoag, and into the corner near the foul line. Three runs scored and Greenberg had himself a stand-up double. Jerry and I jumped out of our seats and hugged one another and the crowd went wild.

Mr. Loudmouth was quiet for the moment.

Greenberg scored when the next batter, Rudy York, singled sharply. Tommy Heinrich, the new Yankee right fielder, scooped up the ball and threw home, but his throw was cut off by Lou Gehrig who saw that Greenberg was already sliding across home plate with the Tigers' fourth run of the inning. When Hank stood up and ceremoniously dusted himself off before returning to the visitors' dugout, the crowd gave him a tumultuous cheer.

Uncle Maxie was pleased: it was only the first inning and his hated Yankees were already losing four to zip.

But the Tigers and Hank Greenberg were not through yet. With none on in the second inning, Greenberg drove his forty-sixth home run deep into the left field stands; then in the seventh, with Charlie Gehringer, the Tiger second baseman on first, he lifted a high fly ball along the left field foul line—fair by inches. The ball bounced into the stands and Hank was held at second base. He would surely have had a triple had it stayed in the field.

When the seventh inning was over, the Tigers were leading 12 to 6. Most of the Yankee fans were starting to leave, including the loudmouth six rows behind us. His parting words, as Greenberg trotted from his position at first base to the dugout to start the eighth inning, were as meaningless as his other pronouncements: "Hey, Greenberg. You got lucky, you fuckin' Jew-boy!"

No one paid much attention to him. Hank Greenberg had already answered him in the best way possible.

But Uncle Maxie suddenly stood up and unleashed a few parting words. "Go to Hell, you big fat dummy!" he shouted, waving the battered yellow-brown straw fedora he always wore to baseball games.

The big fat dummy made a half motion, as if he was going to go after Uncle Maxie, but he turned away and headed toward one of the exits.

Uncle Maxie was delighted with himself and continued waving his hat to others in the stands nearby; they seemed to appreciate his handling of the heckler. It was as if Uncle Maxie did not want his moment of triumph to end. Jerry and I were very proud of him.

The game was completed with no additional scoring. Greenberg grounded out in the top of the ninth and received a standing ovation from the remaining crowd.

Before we got into the subway that would take us home, Uncle Maxie bought Jerry and me orange and black Detroit Tiger pennants, which we carried triumphantly into the bakery.

"We heard," my mother said when she saw us. "Hank hit another home run."

"Yeah, but Uncle Maxie almost got into a fight with a big fat guy," Jerry said.

"Maxie in a fight? What are you talking about?"

And then we told her how this man had called Hank Greenberg all kinds of names and that nobody had answered him back except Uncle Maxie, who had stood up and called him a big fat dummy.

"You're lucky he didn't kill you," my mother said, addressing Maxie, her voice full of emotion.

Then she motioned to him. "Maxie, give me a hand behind the bread counter. We missed you."

When the season ended a month later, Greenberg had hit 58 home runs, two shy of the Babe's record. But none of us in the bakery—or in the entire borough of the Bronx—thought any less of him.

Monday Night Fights

THE BRONX CHEER

For those who may not be familiar with it, a Bronx Cheer is really a jeer, a boo, a vocal expression of derision and ridicule. It is accomplished by wrapping the thumb and forefinger around your lips and blowing out a stream of sound and mist. Because it is such a silly gesture, it is usually followed by laughter. Hence, the "cheer" part.

My father regarded the front window showcase of his bakery store as a most important marketing tool, although he never quite expressed it in that way. He took great pride in carefully arranging displays of butter cookies, babkas, chocolate layer cakes and pies in the front window. Periodically, during the day, he would move them about, adding a fruit pie in place of a butter-cream iced cake that had just been sold, or a tray of fresh Danish pastries where devil's food cakes had been. He took great pains to get things just right, stepping back and squinting now and then like an artist arranging objects for a still life painting.

The only things that marred the beauty of his precious window displays were the posters from the local movie houses or the ones advertising upcoming boxing matches at the Bronx Coliseum, which were placed in one corner of the window. The reason he allowed these intrusions was simple: in exchange for the window space, my father was given free passes to the theaters or fights.

The movie-house passes were quickly claimed by my mother and my aunts, who went to the movies twice each week. Movie going during the Depression years was a great way for adults to forget their troubles. Instead of worrying about where the next rent money would be coming from, they could sit in plush seats in a dark movie theater and be a part of the scene as Melvyn Douglas, in a tuxedo, sipped Champagne with a lavishly gowned and bejeweled Irene Dunne.

My father couldn't have cared less about what Douglas or Dunne or Joan Crawford or Bette Davis, for that matter, were up to; what he craved were the "comps" he received from the Bronx Coliseum, which put on professional matches every Monday night. He figured that if my mother and her sisters were happy with the movie passes, they could not begrudge him free tickets to the fights.

The fact is, these fight posters were garish-looking affairs—usually yellow with huge black and red letters that could be read from across the street. But the tickets were free, and everyone was happy.

Many of the fighters appearing at the Bronx Coliseum were up-and-coming youngsters; they were pitted against some old-timers who should have quit but were hanging on for "one more purse." Occasionally, a champion or a leading contender would come to the Bronx Coliseum for what was termed a "tune-up" for a more important bout, which would be fought a few months later at Madison Square Garden—or occasionally in Yankee Stadium.

My father was always given four tickets to the fights, and he usually went with his two younger brothers, my uncles Ruby and Charley, and Danny Revelis, a salesman from General Mills who sold flour to both my father and Uncle Ruby, who owned a bakery in Brooklyn.

Uncle Charley was the only member of my father's family who was not in the bakery business, having deserted it to become a liquor salesman right after Prohibition was repealed in 1933. Charley lived in

Passaic, New Jersey, and the fights at the Coliseum were his excuse to visit with his brothers. Uncle Charley told funny stories, sang crazy songs like "Yes, We Have No Bananas," and danced a wild Charleston.

Revelis—no one except my mother ever referred to him by his first name—was a widower who had become a quasi member of the family. I liked him because he would defend me in most disputes I had with my father. My father especially liked him because he was awful at the poker games that were played in the back room of the store. Revelis could be counted on to make a major contribution to my father's wallet at these regular sessions.

I was deemed too young to go to the fights. I had only seen one or two from my Aunt Sue and Uncle Morris's apartment, which overlooked Yankee Stadium. From the fire escape on the fifth floor of their apartment building, the male members of the family watched—no tickets necessary—as Jack Sharkey, Max Baer, Jimmy Braddock, Max Schmeling and, of course, Joe Louis made boxing history.

It was quite a sight. Except for the ring area, the entire 70,000-seat stadium was almost totally black. The only lights in the stands would be the flashes of cigars and cigarettes being lit. In the center of the arena, the square ring glistened like a bonfire.

Inside the apartment, the radio's volume was turned up so we could all hear Clem McCarthy, the radio announcer, give his rapid-fire, gravel-voiced, blow-by-blow account of the fight. And through a pair of Uncle Morris's binoculars, which we passed among us, we managed to *almost* see what was happening in the ring.

My chance to see a fight up close came when Revelis stopped by the bakery one Monday afternoon to say that he was not going to be able to make it to the Coliseum that night.

"What's so important?" my father asked. "Tony Canzoneri's fighting tonight. He's a beautiful thing to watch."

"I know, but my daughter-in-law invited me to dinner. I think she's trying to fix me up with an aunt of hers. Maybe you can take the kid in my place," Revelis said, pointing to me. I was sitting at my usual table, near the brass coffee urns, pretending that I wasn't listening, and that I was busy doing my homework.

My father turned to me. "Hey, you wanna go to the fights with me and your uncles?"

"Really? You think Mom will let me?"

"I'll talk to her. It's Tony Canzoneri. He's a little guy, so it won't be bloody."

As my father had predicted, my mother agreed to let me go, provided we didn't come home too late. I was ecstatic. For the rest of the afternoon, it was virtually impossible for me to concentrate on the fractions and long-division problems that I was supposed to conquer before the next day's class.

Around six that evening my uncles arrived, and we all went to the local delicatessen a few doors down from the bakery for a bowl of mushroom barley soup, my favorite. Then, about 7:30, as it grew dark, the four of us walked down to Boston Road and made our way to Tremont Avenue, heading east to the Bronx Coliseum. We looked up. The steep staircases of the nearby elevated train station were crowded with people making their way to the Coliseum. They walked with an intensity and energy that only the prospect of an exciting sporting event can generate.

As we neared the arena, the noise grew louder: people shouted greetings to one another from across the street, newsboys hawked their papers and the peanut vendors were out in force. "Buy 'em here for ten cents. Inside it's a quarter!"

"You wanna bag, kid?" Uncle Ruby asked. "How about some Tootsie Rolls?"

"Stop spoiling him," my father grumbled.

"Since when is a bag a peanuts and some candy spoiling a kid?"

"Since I said so."

"Take it easy, Nate," Uncle Charley chimed in. "It's gonna be a lovely evening." And he started singing "Take Me Out To The Ball Game."

My father sneered at his youngest brother. "Wrong sport, Charley."

Uncle Ruby bought me a bag of peanuts, a Tootsie Roll and a Milky Way. Normally, even one of the three would have been a treat, so I was reveling in my good luck.

Suddenly, there on East 177th Street, in two-foot-high letters, were the words: NEW YORK COLISEUM. Of course, we knew it as the Bronx Coliseum. No one, to my knowledge, ever referred to it otherwise. I was overwhelmed at how beautiful it looked. That night, the Bronx Coliseum—a pink-colored, stucco building with a series of simple arches that encompassed an entire two-block area, a building that would never be confused, architecturally, with the one in Rome—was glittering from giant searchlights that crisscrossed their beams into the sky and across the building's dome. People flocked toward it from every direction until the whole street surrounding it was filled. It was almost like the newsreels of Times Square on New Year's Eve.

"There must be a full house tonight," Ruby said. "Canzoneri's a big draw. What do you think?"

"Twenty thousand?" Charley guessed.

"The place only seats fifteen," my father growled. "So how can you fit twenty?"

"I don't know," Charley mumbled. "But it's a lot for a fight that isn't even for a championship."

My father frowned. "You're always complaining. If you paid for the tickets, you can complain. Otherwise . . . " He was too annoyed to finish.

Ruby interrupted. "I'm hungry."

"How can you be hungry? You just had a big bowl of soup," my father said.

"I'm hungry, too," I said. I hadn't started on the bonanza of goodies that Uncle Ruby had bought for me.

"Let's get to our seats first," my father said.

The seats were great. They were just behind ringside, which was even better than ringside because you didn't have to crane your neck upward to see what was happening in the ring.

Charley beamed. "Great seats, Nate."

"Hey, it was a double-sized poster. Almost covered up half the window," my father said. "For that, they better be good."

As soon as we were seated—me between Ruby and Charley and my father next to Ruby—the ring announcer, who was wearing a tuxedo, just the way announcers did at the big fights in Madison Square Garden or Yankee Stadium, stepped into the center of the ring. With the help of a small megaphone, he directed our attention to two opposite corners of the ring, which were already occupied by the fighters—heavyweights—who had just climbed through the ropes. One of them was wearing a bright black satin robe with the words "Kayo Kennedy" on the back. His entourage of four or five men rubbed his shoulders and arms.

Kayo's opponent looked terrified. Instead of a robe he had a small towel draped around his neck. His single handler shouted in his ear, perhaps offering words of encouragement or some last-minute advice as he patted him on the back.

"This doesn't look like much," Ruby said. "What do you guys want to eat?"

"I'll go with you," I volunteered. I really didn't want to see what Kayo Kennedy was going to do to the frightened young man with the towel.

As we left our seats, Ruby took my hand. "You hold on to me," he said. "I don't want you to get lost."

"Cheezit, Uncle, I'm not a baby. Don't treat me like one," I protested.

"I know you're not a baby, kid, but this is a crazy crowd—and I wouldn't want anything to happen to you," he said quietly. "Okay?"

"Okay, I guess."

We found a concession stand and ordered a half dozen meat sandwiches—roast beef, turkey, corned beef, breast of beef—with extra pickles and a half dozen Coca-Colas. Since the tickets were free, Ruby was going to make sure we all ate well.

I stayed close to him as he cleared a path back to our seats through the crowd. It was a happy bunch, mainly men who, for a buck and a half apiece, could yell and scream like banshees as they watched two guys who probably had never met before try to kill one another.

When we got back to our seats, Charley made it clear that we hadn't missed much. He explained that he had dropped his hat just as the fight had started; by the time he had recovered it, Kayo Kennedy was laid out on the floor of the ring and the referee was in the middle of his ten-count. It seemed that the frightened young man in the towel possessed a crushing left hook that met Kayo's glass jaw. The fight was over before it began.

While we were eating our sandwiches, the announcer introduced the next bout: two overweight heavyweights, both of whom had records that showed more losses than wins. It did not look very promising.

As the fight began, each boxer bobbed and weaved, tossed a few aimless jabs, shuffled around a bit and then clinched until the referee pried them apart. This pattern was repeated two or three times until the crowd started booing. Now the boxers held one another and moved around the ring like two elephants in the Bronx Zoo whose trunks had accidentally become entwined.

The simple boos of frustrated fight fans now became rowdy Bronx cheers.

Suddenly, Uncle Charley, with a corned beef sandwich in one hand and his drink in the other, stood up on his chair and started to sing: "I'll be loving you, always/With a love that's true, always . . . "

This seemed to be the signal for Ruby and my father to stand on their chairs and begin to sing as well: "When the things you've planned/Need a helping hand/I will understand, always . . . "

The slow dance in the ring continued. The fighters would fall back from each other for a couple of seconds, and then they would lurch forward and embrace again. The choreography did not change; neither did the singing of my father and his brothers.

I was thoroughly embarrassed. I wanted to hide. It was bad

enough that they did their Al Jolson and Maurice Chevalier imitations at family gatherings, but this was in front of 15,000 strangers!

Oddly enough, I noticed that everyone around us seemed to be enjoying the sideshow that was being provided by my father and my uncles. Whenever they reached the magical word—*always*—the crowd sang along with them. There was no stopping the brothers now, particularly when the arena lights were directed to shine on them. "Days may not be fair, always/That's when I'll be there, always/Not for just an hour/Not for just a day/Not for just a year, but always."

The fight fans roared their approval. I could hardly believe what I was seeing. My father and my uncles were leading a crowd of half-crazed men, along with a few women, in mocking the performance of two hapless boxers. The brothers simply could not stop; they seemed energized by the crowd's response.

Suddenly, the bell sounded; the referee moved in between the two fighters and mercifully ended the fight. The hysterical crowd gave my father and uncles a standing ovation.

I was no longer embarrassed; in fact, in a strange way, I rather enjoyed the attention that was being showered on them—and me!

Long after the fighting had resumed with other boxers, people in the crowd still smiled and pointed to us. After a while, the pointing and the smiling became a bit unnerving, but there was nothing I could do; anyway, I was having a grand time eating a roast beef sandwich with the extra pickles that Uncle Ruby had supplied.

Finally, it was time for the main event: the great Tony Canzoneri versus a young, inexperienced fighter named Billy Floyd from Utah.

"What the hell is Utah?" my father asked.

"It's a state out West," Ruby replied. "Dempsey came from there. They have their own religion. They're Mormons. The men there can have lots of wives . . . all at the same time."

"Why the hell would they want to do that?" my father asked. "Isn't one enough?"

Charley looked scornfully at my father and pointed to me. "Shh.

Be careful what you say in front of the kid," he cautioned.

"I only meant that one wife is all anyone needs," my father corrected himself. "Right?"

"Right," I said. And we all laughed.

The ring announcer raised his megaphone: "Ladies and gentlemen!" he shouted. "The *main* event!"

The crowd erupted.

"We are honored tonight to have with us a number of celebrities from the world of sports, politics and show business," the announcer bellowed, his voice rising to an ear-splitting crescendo. "Let me introduce the current heavyweight champion of the world—Jimmy Braddock!"

Cheers from the crowd filled the Bronx Coliseum as the much-admired Braddock climbed into the ring and greeted a smiling Tony Canzoneri and a very nervous looking Billy Floyd.

"Great guy," my father said of Braddock.

"Lucky," Ruby said tersely.

"All right," my father said. "Great guy and lucky, too."

After Braddock, the ring announcer brought out the Honorable James J. Lyons, the borough president of the Bronx, who was energetically booed by most of the crowd, including my father. Then came Borah Minnevitch, who was appearing at the Windsor Theatre on Fordham Road with his Harmonica Rascals and, finally, Father Anthony McGuire from St. Thomas Aquinas Church, who blessed both fighters. I wondered how Mr. Floyd, the Mormon from Utah, felt about the Catholic priest's blessings. But perhaps he knew that he was going to need all the help he could get.

I looked at my father and Ruby and Charley, and they were grinning happily. I realized how much fun they were having. I wasn't sure if it was the skills or lack of skills of the boxers that mattered to them as much as the joy that they had in being with one another.

For the first ninety seconds of the fight, the veteran Canzoneri and the neophyte Floyd danced around, "feeling" one another out.

Suddenly, Canzoneri unloaded a series of stunning left jabs, followed by a monstrous right hook that sent young Billy Floyd to the canvas for a quick sleep.

In less than two minutes, the main event was history.

My father and my uncles applauded vigorously.

The crowd, which probably had come to the Coliseum anticipating a quick victory by Canzoneri, seemed relieved that their boy had done his job well and efficiently. Everyone seemed content as they made their way slowly out of the arena.

On the walk back home, my father lit up one of his Between the Acts Little Cigars. He was still smiling as we climbed the three flights of stairs to our apartment.

"Aren't you glad your mother let you come?" he asked.

"It was great," I said.

"Yeah, Canzoneri is a helluva boxer."

"Oh, that was fun. I loved the sandwiches, the peanuts and the Tootsie Roll."

"Yeah. And . . . ?"

"And I liked the way you booed the borough president and cheered Jimmy Braddock."

"Okay."

"But the best part was when Uncle Charley began singing 'Always,' and you and Uncle Ruby got up and started singing with him."

"That *was* funny, wasn't it?" My father grinned at me, then turned his attention to stomping out his cigar stub.

"Yeah," I said. "And I loved it when the spotlight came on all of you, and the whole arena cheered. It was almost like you were on a stage in a theater."

"I guess we're quite an act," my father said, slightly out of breath as he fumbled with the keys to our apartment.

My mother was waiting for us when we walked in.

"So, how were the fights? Did anyone get killed?" she asked.

"No one got killed, and Canzoneri was great," my father said.

"And you should have heard Uncle Charley sing," I piped up.

"What do you mean? Charley sang?"

"And Pop and Uncle Ruby, too. They put spotlights on them, like they were in a theater," I gushed

My mother looked puzzled.

"It's a long story," my father said, winking at me and turning to go into his bedroom.

"Let's go to sleep," he said to my mother. "I gotta fill in for one of the bread bakers at four in the morning."

Comrade Taft

In 1937, a picket line was sacrosanct to almost all residents of the Tremont section of the Bronx. To cross a picket line was to invite bitter hatred from everyone. There were no gray areas. The people on the picket line were right; the people being picketed were wrong. The neighborhood residents lived by this rule, even those who otherwise prided themselves on seeing two or more sides of every issue.

There was room in our community for the religious, the not-so-religious—and even the atheists. You could be a Yankee fan or a Giant fan. You could read the *Daily News* or the *Daily Mirror* in the morning. It didn't matter. But you had to be for *labor*; you had to support, without reservation, any and all union actions.

Strikers were the underdog, the little guy, David against Goliath. What my father feared most in life was a strike by the employees of his bakery; a picket line in front of his store was unthinkable. Accordingly, he worked hard to maintain the best relations he could with the officials who represented the unions with which he dealt: the Bakery and Confectionery Workers Local 1111, and the Retail Salesclerks. My father refused to bake bagels or bialys on his premises, since bagel and bialy bakers were in a different union than the one that represented the bread and cake bakers. Two unions, he figured, were enough for any man. He purchased his bagels and bialys from a wholesale bakery that specialized in those items.

One year, the Teamsters Union tried to organize a unit in my father's store that would consist entirely of John, a Russian alcoholic, who did odd jobs around the bakery. Twice each day, John would wheel a small pushcart containing an assortment of breads, rolls and cakes from the bakery on 180th Street to a small "commission bakery" on Tremont Avenue, three blocks away. It was called a "commission bakery" because it received a twenty percent discount on the products it bought from my father and then resold them at the regular price. The owner supplemented his income by selling newspapers, magazines, cigarettes, candy and milk. Hardly an A&P operation.

My father was irate that someone would consider John's staggering trek up the street the work of a teamster. How could a guy who rolled a pushcart for six blocks be thought of in the same terms as a truck driver?

How my father dealt with the Teamsters on this issue—in 1934— became a family legend.

My father had suggested that the local union official, a heavyset Pole named Stanley, join him for a drink at Mauriello's Bar on Arthur Avenue. There, my father had explained to Stanley that John would be a real burden for the union. Half the time he was drunk; he was often picked up by the police and brought to Fordham Hospital to dry out. "He'd be more trouble than it's worth," my father concluded, certain that his arguments were having some impact on Stanley.

Then, as he reached for his wallet, my father spoke what he thought would be the magic words: "Isn't there some way that we can avoid this situation?"

"As a matter of fact there is," Stanley said, dropping his voice several levels. "Nate, you have a son. Why don't we put *him* in the union? The dues wouldn't cost you much, and he could even come under the union's medical plan."

"My son is only seven years old. How the hell could he be in your union?"

"Who's to know or care?" Stanley asked sweetly.

"Well, somebody might get suspicious if he has to have his tonsils out or gets chicken pox. When was the last time one of your truck drivers filed a claim for that?"

"I see what you mean," Stanley said with a sigh.

"Well, like as I was saying . . . " my father continued, unfolding his wallet. "Maybe this is the best way." He pulled out a $50 bill and started to hand it to Stanley.

"Oh, I think you can do better than that," Stanley said. "I want to buy my wife a new winter coat, the kind with a fur collar."

"Well, get her a new spring coat," my father said.

"Spring it is!" Stanley said with a wide grin and snatched the bill from my father.

Strikes were not an infrequent New York occurrence during the Depression. One day it was the hatters and milliners, next the carpenters or the trolley conductors. Most strikes had no direct effect on my father's business, except that the strikers, without a full paycheck, were not inclined to buy chocolate layer cakes.

When I was ten, my father again had reason to fear a strike or pickets, but this time the threat was coming from the Communist Party. By 1937, the Party probably had more active members in our neighborhood than even the Democrats. My father, who had little use for politicians of any stripe, was convinced that the Communists were determined to make life difficult for anyone engaged in any form of profit-making business.

Accordingly, he kept a low profile when it came to political or social issues. But the Party members were anything but neutral. Each May Day, hundreds of our neighbors—many of my father's customers among them—unfurled tablecloth-sized red flags with the hammer and sickle symbols, and marched before the cheering crowds that lined 180th Street.

There were even some members of our family who professed

Socialist or Communist leanings, and were regular readers of the *Daily Worker.* I was shocked one year when Uncle Menashe's son, Alex, a student at CCNY at the time, described our beloved Franklin D. Roosevelt as a "capitalist stooge."

However, the most admired and outspoken of these left-leaning relatives was Uncle Hagen, who, my father was quick to observe, was not really a relative. Max Hagen was an old and dear friend of my maternal grandparents. They had all met in Yorkville in 1896 while my grandmother was pregnant with my mother. He liked to say he knew her before she was born. Hagen continued to be a part of the family, traveling up to the Bronx twice every week for dinner—Fridays at my grandparents, Tuesdays with us.

Hagen was a fascinating man who had left Germany in the early 1880s with a few possessions, one of which was a well-worn copy of a German translation of Edward Bellamy's *Looking Backward.* He and my father never let their political differences interfere with their pleasure in being together, with good cigars and dark beers.

So it was a surprise when, one Wednesday morning, some days before the Easter and Passover holidays, two high points for the bakery business, my father received a telephone call from Hagen who, of course, he had just seen the night before. Hagen rarely phoned, so my father knew right away that something was wrong. He recounted the call this way:

"Nathan, something's come up. We have to get together," Hagen said.

"What's the matter? You sound like someone died," my father observed.

"Nobody died—yet," Hagen said. "Look, I don't want to talk about this on the phone."

"So why don't you come here? I'll be here all afternoon."

"No, no. We can't be seen together."

"What do you mean 'We can't be seen together'?" My father later admitted that he had raised his voice at that point. "You gone nuts or something?"

My father knew that Hagen was *not* crazy, and agreed to meet him in an hour, which was the length of time it would take my father to get to the Kleine Konditorei in Yorkville. It was near my grandfather's old bakery, where my father had learned his craft. The Kleine Konditorei was one of those places where people could order a coffee and pastry, and sit and talk for hours at a time.

My father found Hagen waiting for him with a freshly poured cup of black coffee and the remains of a streusel crumb cake on a plate before him. Hagen quickly folded his copy of the *Staats-Zeitung und Herald* as my father joined him. "I'm sorry for all the mystery but you'll understand when I tell you," Hagen began.

"Jeezus, Hagen, this better be good."

"That's just it, it's not good," Hagen said, squirming. "I'll get right to it. They're gonna picket your store tomorrow afternoon!"

My father's response, as he would later recall it, went something like this: "What are you talking about? Who's gonna picket my store? We got a contract. It isn't up until next year!" My father's manner was not tranquil. "For this you dragged me downtown? This is nuts!"

"Calm down, Nathan," Hagen said, looking around, to make sure he wasn't being overheard. "The Communists in your neighborhood are organizing a bread strike. They'll be demanding that you cut the price of a loaf of bread from ten to eight cents a pound."

"They gotta be kidding," my father responded. "I'm practically losing money at ten cents. You know we barely make anything on the bread. We sell it cheap so we can get 'em in the store to buy cake."

"I know that, and they know it, too. But who ever heard of a cake strike?"

I can imagine Uncle Hagen smiling as he delivered that line.

"I mean, bread is basic—these guys are not stupid," Hagen continued. "They know that everyone can sympathize with the idea of lowering the price of bread."

"Not if they have to pay for the flour and the salaries of the bakers," my father countered. Then he asked Uncle Hagen how he knew about the planned strike.

Uncle Hagen told him that shortly before he had telephoned, he had heard that there had been a meeting at the Party's storefront on Mohegan Avenue. The local Party head, Taft, had pushed for a quick action against shopkeepers before the holidays, which was when the small merchants did their best business, and would be the most vulnerable if there was to be a strike. The two prime targets, he was told, boiled down to my father and Buckholz, the butcher.

My father moaned. "So let 'em go after Buckholz. Why me?"

"Because Buckholz is one of them," Hagen informed him. "He gives a lot to the Party."

My father wasn't often surprised, but this bit of news took the wind out of him. "Buckholz's a Communist? Can't be. He's the biggest thief on the block. He'd sooner screw one of his customers than his wife. He's got his thumb on the scale every time he fills an order."

"Well, he and his sons are all Communists. So you're *it*," Hagen replied. He leaned back in his chair and drew out a leather cigar case from his pocket. He offered a cigar to my father, who waved it away. "I got a call this morning from one of the guys who was at the meeting. He feels terrible about it, but there is nothing he can do. He says Taft's trying to make a name for himself downtown, and this is as good a way as any."

After a few seconds or so, my father reached into his own jacket for his tin of Between the Acts Little Cigars. Finally, he looked up at Hagen. "Do I know this guy, Taft?"

"Yes," Hagen said quickly. "He's been coming to the store for years. Very tough looking guy; used to be a truck driver. But he's very smart."

"Good. If he's smart, I can talk to him," my father said.

"If you mean, paying him off," Hagen countered, "it isn't going to happen. Taft is dedicated to the Party. He's a very principled man. He'd never . . ."

"I remember him now—short, stocky guy with a red face and long white hair. Always tries to feel up the salesgirls. Thinks he's hot shit."

"I'm telling you, Nathan, you try to bribe him, you'll really drive him wild. No telling what he'll do."

Much later, my father told me that, once he had been able to visualize Taft, he believed he could handle him. It was at that point that he lit up his cigar. Then he asked Uncle Hagen to arrange an appointment for him to meet with Taft that evening.

Uncle Hagen walked to one of the phone booths near the restrooms to make the call. When he returned, he announced: "Six o'clock at Dominick's. He likes their Yankee Bean soup."

"Good," my father responded. "Already he wants me to buy him dinner."

Before my father left the Kleine Konditorei, Uncle Hagen warned him again: "Taft doesn't care about money. He really cares about his people."

My father smiled. "I'll get him to care for *me*. After all, I'm people, too."

When I finished school that day, I walked over to the bakery and sat down at one of the rear tables. I placed a bottle of milk and a glass in front of me, with a cinnamon bun that had escaped the morning rush, and proceeded to try to do my homework. I was glad to have my father interrupt me. "Your mother has to take your sister to the doctor tonight, so you and I are going out for dinner," he said.

"Really? That sounds great," I said, swallowing some milk. "Is Edith sick or something?"

"Just a sore throat, but your mother thought it was best if the doctor looked at her," he said. "She's fine, really."

I was excited. Going out to dinner was a real treat. I hoped I could order lamb chops, because they came with little paper boots so you didn't dirty your fingers when you wanted to chew on the bones.

We left the bakery about 5:30 and took the 180th Street trolley to Third Avenue. I was really impressed when I saw Dominick's Oyster & Chop House. It was a long, narrow place with a bar up front, two rows of tables on each side, and mirrors that stretched the whole length of the restaurant. The bar area was crowded with men, chatting and laughing with the two bartenders.

A man, who I assumed was the owner or manager, approached us as we entered. He smiled.

"We'll be three for dinner," my father said.

"I see," said the man as he led us to a table midway into the restaurant. "I gather your guest has not arrived yet."

"No, I guess not," my father said, glancing quickly at the mostly empty tables. "He's a short fellow, with long white hair."

"Ah, you mean Taft?"

"Yes," my father said. "Does he come here often?"

"You might say it's his home away from home. Johnnie Walker Black and prime ribs of beef. We're all fond of Taft—a generous man."

I was surprised that I was not having dinner alone with my father. "Who's this guy, Taft?" I asked, showing some annoyance along with my curiosity. "You never said there would be another person."

"I knew you wouldn't want to come if I told you, but I want you to be here with me. It's important. I don't want you to say anything. Just eat and listen. Maybe you'll learn something."

My father looked up at the wall clock. Six on the button.

A waiter appeared with menus.

"We'll be three," my father said.

"I know," he said with a smile. "Friends of Taft. He may be a little late, if I know Taft. Would you like to order a drink for yourself and the young man?"

"Of course," said my father, "Johnnie Walker Black."

"Ah, Taft's drink." The waiter nodded.

"I guess so."

The waiter turned toward me. "Coca-Cola? Ginger ale?"

"Celery tonic," I said.

"I'm afraid it's Coca-Cola or ginger ale," the waiter said, continuing to smile.

"Just water, please," I answered glumly.

It was obvious to me that the whole dinner was not going right. They didn't have celery tonic, and instead of it being just the two of us, now there was going to be a white-haired guy named Taft. And what kind of a name was that?

After our drinks arrived, and the smiling waiter left us, my father started talking to me again. "Remember what I told you. You are just to sit there and listen. Even if he talks to you, don't answer. Make believe you're stupid. I know you're smart but play dumb. This turns out right, next Tuesday afternoon we'll go to the Polo Grounds. The Giants are playing the Dodgers."

I was placated and somewhat curious now.

About a quarter after six, there was a flurry of excitement in the bar area of the restaurant, and a moment later Taft appeared at our table. He was as advertised: short and stocky with a shock of long white hair that drifted over his forehead, and a strutting walk like James Cagney in a gangster movie. He wore a dark gray pinstriped suit that I thought fit too snugly. He extended his hand, which sparkled with a diamond pinkie ring, and produced a smile. "As you can guess," he said, "I'm Taft, and you are . . . "

"Nathan, or just call me Nate," my father answered. "And this is my son. I had to bring him along because my wife had to take our daughter to the doctor. I hope you don't mind."

"It's fine with me," Taft said. "After all, I am here at your request."

"That's true. But before we talk business, let's have dinner."

"Fine with me." Taft seated himself across from my father. "I'll join you in a drink, if I may?"

My father signaled for the waiter. "My friend here will have a Johnnie Walker Black, no ice, chilled."

"How'd you know that?" Taft asked.

"Oh, you'd be surprised what I know about you, Taft." My father grinned, giving me a broad wink. As far as I knew, all my father knew about Taft was that he drank Johnnie Walker Black and that he liked prime ribs of beef.

The conversation at dinner didn't reveal much more, at least to me. I found out that Taft liked the horses—he went to Saratoga Springs to watch the thoroughbreds race every August. At one point, Taft called the waiter over and asked him to bring him a pack of Camels. The waiter brought them; Taft handed him a folded dollar bill and waved his hand when the waiter said he would bring him change. I was surprised because I didn't think cigarettes cost more than fifteen cents a pack, even in a spiffy place like Dominick's. I wondered if Mr. Taft was a very rich man or just a very generous one.

For dessert, I ordered my favorite—chocolate pudding. My father and Taft had apple pie a la mode, my second-favorite dessert.

As they were finishing their slices of pie, the waiter brought them coffee. My father pulled out two large cigars and offered one to Taft, who accepted it with barely a nod of thanks. I was trying to read my father's mind, but he was revealing nothing.

"Okay, Taft," my father said softly. "What's this I hear, there is going to be a strike at Buckholz's butcher shop—and just before the holidays? I don't think that's right. Buckholz barely makes a living in that place, and this coming week is one of the biggest of the year. If you strike his place, how's he gonna keep giving you money?"

Taft looked shocked. "What do you mean by that? Are you saying that Buckholz gives me money?"

"Not *you* personally," my father quickly explained. "I mean to the Party."

"Oh, I thought . . . " Taft stumbled over his words. "But you got everything mixed up. For your information, we are planning to put up a picket line in front of *your* store, Nate." Taft smiled slyly. "We want you to cut your bread prices from ten cents to eight cents a pound. People are starving, you know."

"I know," said my father. "That's why I only charge a dime. I should really be charging fifteen cents a pound, but it would drive everybody away, and no one would buy any cakes or pies."

"Well, there's nothing I can do. We voted yesterday to have a picket line in front of your place tomorrow afternoon. I can't go against my executive committee."

"I think you can," my father said. He pulled out a small pad he kept in his jacket. "It's simple arithmetic. If I take in less money, then in order to survive, I have to give my bakers less. And since I can't give them less under their union contract, I have to have less bakers." He looked sternly at Taft. "You follow me?"

Without waiting for a reply, my father continued in non-stop fashion, writing everything onto his pad. "See, I sell about four hundred and eighty loaves of bread every day. That's thirty-three hundred, give or take a few, each week. Now, if I take off two cents for each loaf, as you want me to do, that would cost me $67 each week. That's almost two bread bakers I gotta cut. I don't think Local 1111 would be happy about that. Especially when I have to tell 'em that some fancy-Dan Communist is forcing me to do this so he can be a big shot with his goddamn executive committee." My father said all of this without raising his voice.

Taft started to say something but my father was too quick for him. "You see, everything has consequences. For you to be a big shot, you gotta trash me, and for me to stay ahead of the game, I have to fire two bakers, and they go to the union, who comes after me until I tell 'em that you—Comrade Taft—are at the bottom of it all."

My father tried to take a puff on his cigar, which, unfortunately, had gone out during his tirade against Taft.

Taft folded his arms around his chest. I saw that there was a thin layer of sweat on the part of his forehead not covered by his white hair. "I . . . I . . . uh . . . I see what you mean," he mumbled. He didn't seem as suave or as confident as he'd been earlier. "But I don't know . . . I really don't think I can stop this . . . you know, there's my executive committee . . ."

"I notice you say *my* executive committee. Well, if they're *your* executive committee, they'll do what *you* want 'em to do."

"It's not that simple," Taft whined.

"I'll make it very simple for you," my father said. He reached inside his jacket, pulled out his wallet and placed it on the table. "If I ain't mistaken, there's a fifty-dollar bill in here somewhere. In fact, two fifties." He ran his fingers along the edges of dozens of cards and pieces of paper until he found some bills. "Ah, here we are. Two brand-new fifty-dollar bills that will make it easy for you to persuade your *exec-u-tive com-mit-tee* to forget about picketing my store."

My father had pulled apart the syllables of the words "executive committee" with more sarcasm in his voice than I'd ever heard him use before.

"I wouldn't normally accept this from you, Nate, but I want to do what's right," Taft replied.

"Of course," my father said, maintaining a straight face.

Taft quickly pocketed the two fifty-dollar bills, and then he spoke slowly: "I know you're friendly with Hagen, and, if I may ask, I would like you to do one thing for me. Don't tell him I took this. Okay?"

"Absolutely. But on one condition. Don't ever try this on me again."

"Right."

Taft slid out of his chair and turned and walked out of the restaurant.

My father relit his cigar, blew several perfect smoke rings and called for the check.

Taft was true to his word: the next day, no pickets paraded in front of my father's bakery demanding a cut in the price of a loaf of bread.

I was already in the bakery the next afternoon when Uncle Hagen stopped in before going to dinner at my grandfather's. He was in a cheerful mood as he sat down at the table where I was licking the icing off the top of a chocolate éclair and my father was smoking one of his usual little cigars.

"I didn't call again because I got the good news yesterday morning," Uncle Hagen said. "My friend called me and said that Taft and the executive committee had a change of heart, and they decided, politically, that this was not a good time to have a bread strike.

They're planning a big recruitment thing before May Day."

"Good," my father said.

"You see?" Uncle Hagen continued. "All you had to do was explain your situation to him and he would understand. He said he enjoyed his dinner with you. What else did you all talk about?"

"Oh, a little of this, a little of that. I can't remember," my father said with a smile. "The kid was there, maybe he can tell you what went on."

I looked up from my éclair, which was now clean of any chocolate icing. "Yeah, I can tell you. Taft and Pop had Johnnie Walker Black. Taft had Yankee Bean soup and prime ribs of beef. Pop had a half dozen clams on the half shell and roast chicken. I had split pea soup and lamb chops and chocolate pudding. Then Pop gave him two fifty-dollar bills and told him to forget about picketing the store. He begged Pop not to tell you about it. I guess he was kind of embarrassed."

Hagen slumped in his chair. He kept shaking his head. "I always thought he was different . . . a very principled man."

"I guess you were wrong," my father said. "Frankly, I didn't know what to expect when I asked you to arrange a meeting with Taft. Maybe he was, as you thought, really concerned about people." My father put his arm gently on Hagen's shoulder. "But, you know, going after somebody like me is not exactly like going after J. P. Morgan or General Motors. I figured him for a bully. And bullies are never a problem."

Hagen sighed and made a helpless gesture.

"Hey, forget it," my father concluded. "Let's celebrate. I got a couple of cold Michelobs in the icebox."

I don't think Uncle Hagen forgot it, and I didn't, either. I never saw Taft come into the bakery again, but every once in a while I would see him around the neighborhood. He was usually sounding off, making himself into a big shot. But then he would catch a glimpse of me out of the corner of his eye, and his expression would change just a bit. I wonder if he really recognized me or if it was just my imagination.

Fire Sale

One evening in April, 1938, when I was eleven, a mysterious fire broke out in the basement of the paint store next to our family's bakery. The fire spread rapidly, and within minutes there was a huge explosion, which demolished the paint store and blew away a good portion of one side of our bakery.

Luckily, it occurred after the night counterman, my Uncle Phil, and Betty Russo, one of the salesclerks, had already closed up shop. The night shift of bakers did not normally come to work until after midnight. So, except for a family of cats who patrolled the cellar area where the baking was done, the store was empty.

A customer who lived across the street from the bakery heard the explosion and the fire engines, and telephoned my mother to tell her what was happening. It was a Tuesday night, and my father, who played pinochle at his club in Yorkville on Tuesdays, was already on his way home. My mother scrawled a note to him, which she attached to the icebox with some adhesive tape, grabbed hold of my sister, Edith, and me, and ran as fast as she could to the bakery. I wondered how my father would react when he read the harsh words: THE STORE IS ON FIRE.

Before we even got to the bakery, we could hear the commotion:

the roar of the water hoses, the shouts of the firemen and policemen and the excited comments of the neighbors and customers who had gathered across the street. There was little else we could do except join the crowd and watch the frightening scene that was playing out before us.

I turned away for a moment and saw that my mother was crying. It was not like her to cry. The last time I could recall her doing so was when my grandmother had died.

We were there for well over an hour before my father finally showed up. By then the fire had been contained, the crowds had gone home and the traffic was flowing again.

The next morning we learned that the fire and the subsequent explosion had destroyed the concrete firewall that ran the length of the bakery and separated it from the paint store. The firewall at least had done its job of preventing the total destruction of the bakery. The staircase leading down to the ovens and the wooden dumbwaiter that brought the finished products up from the cellar were beyond repair and would have to be replaced before the bakery could open again. But fortunately, neither of my father's precious brick ovens in the cellar was damaged.

Each of us was affected in a variety of ways by the fire and the temporary closing of the bakery.

My mother suddenly found herself, as she put it, "a lady of leisure." She went shopping with her cousin Janet from Brooklyn but was unable to bring herself to buy anything, and then she went to see a matinee performance of *Our Town*. She said that she cried from the moment it started until the curtain fell. (My mother was doing a great deal of crying that particular week.) She even went to the Metropolitan Museum of Art one afternoon with her friend, Eva, who was considered the intellectual in her crowd.

But a few days later, she confessed to me that she missed the bakery. Maybe not the bakery, per se, but rather the attention she received on a daily basis from the salesclerks and the bakers, and from many of the customers, who addressed her as "Mrs. K."

Somehow, the salesclerks at A&S didn't seem to notice her at all.

Deprived of my favorite table at the bakery, I tried a number of substitute places in which to spend my after-school hours, but none of them provided me with milk and devil's food cake. The benches along the south entrance to the Bronx Zoo proved to be the best of the lot. At least there was a place to sit and a passing scene lively enough to keep me from concentrating too deeply on my *Wonders of Science* textbook.

My father was the one most affected by the fire. His immediate concern was, of course, money. Fortunately, the insurance policy of my father's landlord would cover the physical damage to the bakery, but even while the bakery was shut, my father would need cash to continue to support his family, pay various suppliers and make certain that a few of his employees, who could not rely on their unions for help during the time the bakery would be closed, would not go hungry.

Freddie Martinez was one such employee whom my father wanted to take care of. Ostensibly a porter, Freddie was in reality my father's indispensable right-hand man. Whatever it took, my father was determined to keep Freddie on salary.

While the bakery was a successful business, small retail shops like my father's operated from day to day. Even a week without income could be devastating. There was no plump cushion of savings to fall back on. Mr. Newman, the manager of the local Chase Bank on Southern Boulevard, could be counted on to help, but my father confessed to my mother that he knew that he would need a great deal more than the good will he had established with his suppliers to keep from going under. He figured Uncle Morris might come through with a short-term loan.

Of course, that was just the money part. The bakery itself was the center of my father's life, and suddenly he was off on the sidelines with nothing to do. He felt angry, too, because he was certain that the fire had been set deliberately by the owner of the paint store, a recent émigré from Poland named Minka. He had heard from

Schulman our landlord, who was also Minka's landlord, that the poor fellow had been behind in his rent for two months, and that some of his suppliers were already demanding "cash-on-delivery."

Obviously, the man was having serious financial difficulties, and it was not uncommon during the Depression for a failing business to suddenly go up in smoke so that the owner could collect insurance money.

"Maybe he thought a small fire might get him a few dollars," Schulman mused.

"Whoever heard of a small fire in a paint store?" my father growled. "I hope they nail the bastard!"

Soon, my father's anger changed to frustration. He was used to working ten or twelve or even fourteen hours every day, except on Tuesday afternoons when he went to the racetrack with his brother, Ruby, and then to his pinochle game in the evening. Now, his regular routine of work and play was completely disrupted.

During that first week after the fire, my father spent most of his time trying to clean up whatever had not been rendered useless. There was a considerable amount of water damage, particularly in the cellar area. Freddie Martinez and Uncle Menashe, who was actually my great-uncle, came to help, but there was little they could do to advance the opening of the bakery, at least not until a new firewall was in place and the dumbwaiter and the staircase had been rebuilt.

In the meantime, Schulman had hired his brother-in-law, who ran one of the largest—and most politically well-connected—construction companies in the Bronx, to undertake the repair job. They estimated it would take about six weeks to complete.

"Six weeks! Are they nuts?" my father screamed when Schulman told him. "What do they think they're building? Grand Central Station?"

"Take it easy, Nate," Schulman said. "Lou's the best in the business. He's gonna do what has to be done, and your stuff comes first. He figures he'll have everything enclosed in a few days—four or five tops. He'll put up a temporary staircase, a new dumbwaiter, and you can be back in business in three weeks."

"Three weeks? I guess I can live with that," my father grumbled. "I just hope I don't lose any of my guys. Friedhoffer's been after my cake baker for years."

Like everyone else, Schulman knew that Friedhoffer was my father's big rival. Schulman tried to assure my dad that his chief baker would not desert him. "You talking about Gustaf?" Schulman asked. "Don't worry about him. He loves working in your shop. Tell him to take his vacation now." Then he looked off to the side, as if to see if anyone, besides me, was listening. "If you need some money, I can let you have a couple a hundred now, and maybe a little more after my insurance money kicks in."

That last offer seemed to placate my father, but that night he told my mother that he was beginning to wonder if, perhaps, Schulman might have had a hand in the fire, too. It was a little too cozy. Maybe Schulman was in cahoots with his brother-in-law in a scheme to defraud the insurance company? After all, why—suddenly and without being asked—was Schulman offering to lend my father money so he could hold on to Gustaf, his cake baker?

My father had never liked Schulman. Not because he was his landlord—he understood that someone had to be the landlord—but he felt that Schulman was a bit of a shark, both in business and in personal matters. A few years before, there had been a dispute between them regarding a point in the bakery's lease, and my father had had to threaten to go to court in order get Schulman to agree to what was clearly my father's right. But that was business, and my father could understand that.

What he could not accept was Schulman's obvious and insatiable womanizing. The landlord was a remarkably handsome man and he knew it. As a result, there was not a female salesclerk in the bakery who was safe from his eyes or hands.

"If he has to squeeze something," my father once said, "let him squeeze his tomatoes." This was a reference to the fact that, in addition to renting out the group of stores, of which my father's bakery was one, Schulman ran a huge fruit and vegetable market that was located on the other side of the now-destroyed paint store.

There were additional reasons that my father suspected that his landlord might have had something to do with the fire. One evening at dinner, my mother mentioned that she had seen Schulman's wife near the fur department at Lord & Taylor's. "She was buying a new coat. How many fur coats does that woman need?" my mother asked.

"Who knows?" my father said. "Every time he gets a new girl-friend, he has to buy his wife a new coat."

"Well, this time she said he had just made a big business deal, and they could afford a new coat."

"Big business deal? Is that what he calls it?" My father raged. "You know something, our Mr. Schulman could be a crook. How come all the damage from the fire was on my side of the paint store, and he gets off scot-free?"

It was true. Strangely enough, there had been minimal damage done to Schulman's produce market. He didn't miss a day's business. All the serious damage had been to the paint store and to the part of my father's bakery that abutted it.

Of course, there was little my father could do or say about his suspicions beyond voicing his opinion at home. When he saw Schulman a few days later, he simply complained about how helpless he felt as he watched the slow progress of the contractors.

"Listen to me, Nate," Schulman declared. "My brother-in-law knows what he's doing. Why don't you take a rest for a week?"

"Rest?" my father yelled. "How can I rest?"

"So don't rest. Go to the track. Go to a baseball game. Go to a movie. Just leave these guys alone," Mr. Schulman insisted.

The next day my father slept late. He didn't get up until 6:30 in the morning. It was the first time I ever remember having breakfast with him. It was not a pleasant experience. He complained that the coffee was too weak and that the rolls were tasteless. My mother said that was the way she liked her coffee; as for the Kaiser rolls, she explained, "They came from The Butter Cup. Where else am I going to get them?"

The Butter Cup was a bakery on Tremont Avenue, a few blocks from my father's store. It was never really serious competition for my father. "Be grateful that they aren't as good as the ones you make," she said. "In a few weeks, when you open up again, your old customers will really appreciate your rolls."

"Yeah, maybe you're right," he said, smiling for just a brief moment.

"You have to look at the bright side," my mother concluded.

That Tuesday afternoon, my father went with his brother to Belmont Racetrack. He was determined to forget the bakery and concentrate on charting the horses. He needed to enjoy himself.

As usual, he was a cautious, conservative bettor, putting what he called "science" over intuition. He placed his money on the favorites while Uncle Ruby bet long shots. For six races my father had invested $36—a bit of a comedown from his usual amounts. He actually won three of the races but he still was out $12. He sadly reported this information to us at dinner that night.

Uncle Ruby, it seemed, had bet $10 on each race and while he won only one time, his winning bet had been on a 30-to-one shot, so he ended up ahead by $240. This, of course, had further enraged my father who, in desperation, had gone against everything he believed and wagered on a couple of long shots in the final two races—neither of which came close to winning.

"It's all because of you that I lost those last two races," he had ranted at his brother. As long as my father wasn't working, nothing else seemed to work, either.

After dinner, instead of going on to his pinochle club in Yorkville, my father decided to take Schulman's advice, and we all went to the movies. The Loew's Elsmere was showing *Boys Town* with Spencer Tracy and Mickey Rooney. Tracy, along with James Cagney, George Raft and Paul Muni, was among the few movie stars that my father admired. However, Tracy's presence failed to compensate for the rest of the film, which my father found "unbelievable, boring—and nothing with nothing."

It was not a good week.

Two days later, it looked as if my father's luck had changed when Ruby telephoned to ask if he could help him out. Two of my uncle's bread bakers had called in sick and he was desperate for some help.

"One guy out, I can handle," Ruby exclaimed. "But two guys at the same time is a problem, particularly with Easter Sunday only a couple a days away."

"You don't have to rub it in," my father said bitterly. "Bad enough I'm going nuts doing nothing, but I'm missing a big holiday, too."

"Yeah, well I'm sorry I brought up Easter, but whatta ya say? Can you come to Brooklyn and give me a couple days? You don't even have to go home; you can stay with Beattie and me."

"Of course I'll come," my father replied. "But don't trouble Beattie. I don't mind the subway."

The next day, my father was at his brother's bakery in Brooklyn at six in the morning. There was a mound of dough sitting on one of the workbenches waiting to be made into Kaiser rolls. My father grabbed an apron and wrapped it around his waist; for the next four hours, he happily mixed up batches of dough, shaped rolls and chatted about the horses with two of Ruby's bakers. They knew that he was their boss's brother, and they treated him with appropriate respect.

All went well until my father told one of Ruby's bakers that he did not like the way he used the roll press, a device that divided a mound of dough into twelve equal parts, each one big enough to shape into a roll. "You're coming down too hard on that press," my father declared. "You're not breaking rocks, you know."

The Brooklyn baker looked at his partner but he didn't respond. Instead he came down on the press harder than before.

"What are you, some kind of wise guy?" my father shouted. "You can take your apron off and just get the hell outta here."

Unfortunately, both of Ruby's bakers decided it was time to leave. Ruby caught them on the way out and convinced them to come back to work. My father finished up his day's work at Ruby's shop, but it was agreed between the two brothers that perhaps it would be best if my father didn't come to help the next day.

This is how it went for my father for the rest of the week: mornings he visited the bakery and with Freddie's help did what little cleaning up he could do; in the afternoons he paid a solitary visit to Belmont—without his brother who was, of course, busy working at his own shop.

My father's evenings were divided between taking my mother to the movies, which made him more irritable than ever, and his pinochle club, where he bumped into Mr. Friedhoffer who, as expected, asked him how Gustaf was doing. My father was delighted to tell him that Gustaf had gone on an early vacation with his family to Atlantic City and couldn't wait to get back to work in my father's bakery.

As for the movies, the parts that interested my father the most were the newsreels, featuring scenes of labor unrest in the West Virginia coal mines and a frightening display of Hitler's armies, which had parked themselves along the Czech border. At least, he said, there was something real about *those* pictures.

That Saturday, I visited the bakery with my father. It had been twelve days since the fire. There seemed to be genuine progress with the new firewall. The temporary staircase was already set up and a new dumbwaiter had been installed. That morning three workmen came by to adjust the ropes and pulleys that would enable it to go up and down. It seemed to me that it was only a matter of days before my father would return full-time to his bakery; then perhaps the rest of us could relax.

The following Monday, I decided I'd had enough of the benches outside the zoo, and I returned to doing my homework at the rear table in the bakery. There was something almost eerie about the empty store. It was not unpleasant, but I missed the hustle and bustle that I was accustomed to.

I was busy reading about Peter Stuyvesant's purchase of Manhattan Island from the Indians when I saw my father coming up from the cellar on the new, temporary staircase, accompanied by three men. Two of them were dressed in neat, dark blue uniforms, which gave them a rather imposing demeanor; the other, by contrast, walked hunched over in an ill-fitted, rumpled, gray business suit.

They took one of the tables farthest from where I was sitting. I couldn't hear what they were saying, but I could see that they were passing various sheets of paper to my father and he was reading them carefully before signing them.

Freddie Martinez sidled up to where I was sitting. "Fire marshals," he murmured. 'They think Minka deliberately set the fire. They came a couple hours ago, and your Pop's been takin' 'em around."

All I could say was, "Wow!"

"Keep your voice down," Freddie whispered. "The little guy is from the insurance company."

"Why do they think it was arson?" I asked.

"Who said anything about arson?" Freddie growled.

"Well, you said these guys think Minka started the fire. That's arson."

"All right, so it's arson," Freddie said. "There's also a bit of fraud, too. It seems that the bill Schulman sent to the insurance company for the work that his brother-in-law is doing is way outta line. That's what tipped them off that something was not right."

It was all quite fascinating to me, and Freddie seemed pleased to have someone to talk to about it.

"So why are they questioning my father?" I asked nervously.

"They're trying to get a line on Schulman—you know, how he runs his business. They told your Pop right off that they figure he had nothin' to do with it because he ain't making a dime outta the fire. In fact, he's taking a beating, as far as money is concerned."

"Money is only half of it. He's driving himself crazy," I said.

"And he's takin' it out on me," Freddie groaned. "The man's gotta work. He's gotta be yelling at somebody. He ain't happy unless something's going wrong, and he's there to fix it."

By the end of the week we found out that Schulman already had leased the space where the paint store had been to a brand-new dairy, and that the rent would be almost ten percent more than he had been charging Minka. As far as my father was concerned, there was no justice.

But Schulman had done one thing right. His brother-in-law might have been fast and loose with his billing practices, but he knew his business and managed to get the reconstruction of the bakery done in record time. It appeared that it would be only a matter of days before we'd be open for business; there was a chance that my father would not lose another weekend.

The next day, my father took me to a sign store on Third Avenue, where we picked up two large cardboard signs that he had ordered—one announced the reopening of the bakery, and the other a special sale on Kaiser rolls: BUY A DOZEN—GET A HALF-DOZEN FREE! It was my father's way of reminding his customers, who had been forced to buy their rolls at The Butter Cup, just how good his rolls were, both in taste *and* price.

Freddie and I were enlisted to tape the signs to the window while my father stood outside on the sidewalk, supervising the work. The signs were difficult to handle, and my father insisted that they be lined up perfectly straight with one another but not block the display of cakes that would eventually fill the window.

"Move it up on the right side," he ordered. "The *right* side, not the left. Do I have to do it myself?"

We tried to do what he asked, but he never seemed to understand that his right was our left, and vice versa. What we could see, though, was his face, which had become a bright shade of pink; the veins in his neck looked as if they were about to burst.

"He's happy," Freddie whispered to me. "He's so happy to be yelling again. Once the bakers come in tomorrow, he'll have a whole army to scream at. He'll be in heaven."

The following day, a Friday, exactly twenty days after the fire, the bakery reopened. It was as if it had never been closed. The customers were back in droves.

Freddie told me that by nine o'clock that morning my father had already brought one of the salesclerks to tears for using a No. 6 bag for a small rye bread when a No. 4 would have been large enough.

He had yelled at one of the bread bakers, even threatened to punch him, because a half-empty 80-pound bag of flour had not been properly tied up before being placed back on the storage shelf.

By noon, he had argued vociferously with his favorite bakery supply salesman because his price on egg yolks was nine cents more per quart than before the fire.

And he had sneered contemptuously at a customer who'd had the nerve to change her mind about how many prune Danish she wanted to buy.

My mother had carefully avoided him as he hustled from the cellar to the store. "Stay out of his way," she'd warned her sisters, Bertha and Sylvia, who were working with her behind the sales counters. "He's really on a tear. It's like he's had three weeks of screaming all bottled up, and now he's letting it out on everyone."

My father, by all accounts, was impossible for most of that first day. In a matter of three weeks, he had gone from being a tough, often lovable, taskmaster to being an angry, frustrated and bored misanthrope. He had spent this first morning and afternoon at his reopened bakery letting off steam.

Around four o'clock in the afternoon, just before the evening rush, I watched him as he stood quietly in front of the bread and rolls display counter and lit one of his favorite small cigars. He did so slowly, with great relish and ceremony. Then he turned and smiled at me.

"Listen," he said, "go find Freddie. I need you two to take down that crazy sign about giving away six free rolls for each dozen." He paused for a moment and actually chuckled. "Really," he said, "they're lucky to have us back. There's no reason for us to give away the store."

Minka was never charged with arson.

Schulman's bill to the insurance company for the work done by his brother-in-law was cut in half.

And Mrs. Schulman had to return her fur coat to Lord & Taylor's. She told my mother she didn't like the color.

Last Rites?

Both my father and grandfather had little use for organized religion, believing that a person's relationship with God was a deeply personal matter. Still, they went out of their way to see to it that the bakery maintained excellent relations with the churches and the synagogues in the area. It was simply a matter of good business.

This meant that my grandfather served on the board of the synagogue that was closest to the bakery, Congregation Ahavas Sholom Anshei Sfard on East 178th Street, and that my father would deliver, personally, boxes of cookies to the minister of Beck's Memorial Presbyterian Church, which was located at 980 East 180th Street, down the block and across the street from the bakery.

My grandfather found his close association with the synagogue a chore, and eventually my father was given the double whammy of dealing with the rough-and-tumble Orthodox synagogue along with the somewhat staid Presbyterian church.

Frankly, he much preferred Beck's—and with good reason. Rabbi Jonah Horowitz at Ahavas Sholom would never let up on the family's failure to attend services except for perfunctory appearances during Rosh Hashanah and Yom Kippur. On the other hand, Rev. Leslie Turner, of Beck's Memorial Presbyterian, never suggested that my father change either his ways or his religion. He always accepted his weekly box of cookies and the cache of hot cross buns on Good Friday with enormous gratitude. He lavished almost sermon-like praise on the superior quality of their taste.

In addition, my father appreciated the fact that this business of giving was not a one-way street. My mother could always expect a bottle of Harvey's Bristol Cream Sherry at Christmastime from Rev. Turner, and my father would receive a bottle of J&B Scotch.

Rev. Turner could be counted on to visit the bakery at least once a day: in the morning for a cup of coffee and a sweet roll, and sometimes in the afternoon for a Danish or a slice of pound cake. Somehow, in spite of these daily treats, he maintained the lean look of an athlete. It was during his afternoon visits that I would see him. He called me "young man," from the time I was eight or nine. Even after I was married and the father of two daughters my title stayed the same. Except for his formal greeting, he was easier to talk to and more accessible to me than most of my father's friends.

What particularly endeared the reverend to my father, besides the fact that they never discussed religion, was that Rev. Turner loved sports and card playing. The good minister followed baseball assiduously; he was a wizard at hearts and poker; he knew the name of the current bantamweight champion (something only boxing fanatics were aware of); and he was passionate about horse racing although he personally never bet.

One afternoon, when I arrived at the bakery after school, I found these two good friends in what appeared to be deep conversation. Coffee cups and a plate with the remains of a prune Danish were on top of the centerfold of *The Morning Telegraph*, the racing fan's "bible." I figured that Rev. Turner and my father were discussing the possible winner of the sixth race at Pimlico or some such weighty problem, so I simply seated myself at the other end of the table and prepared to enjoy my afternoon snack, a chocolate brownie and some milk. I really wasn't that interested in the fact that the favorite was possibly carrying too much weight or that it had been assigned the post-position farthest from the rail. But I was surprised to realize that my father wasn't really engaged in the conversation, either.

"You're not concentrating, Nate," Rev. Turner said. "Didn't you hear me say that I think it's wrong for a big stable like Greentree to put an apprentice in an important stakes race?" He paused for a moment, and then tried again. "Are you okay?"

"Yeah . . . well . . . not really. I hardly slept last night."

"Business that bad?"

"No, that's not it." My father spoke softly, clearly aware that my eyes had wandered off my civics textbook and that I was tuned in to his conversation with Rev. Turner. "The real problem is that we're trying to bring over one of Lilly's cousins to America. I don't have to tell you how bad things are in Germany for the Jews."

"I'm well aware of the situation," Rev. Turner said. "My church is involved in trying to bring over some of the artists and intellectuals, Christians as well as Jews."

"Well, this is just a kid. Not some famous professor. He's all of 19, you know." My father sighed. "He was studying to be a chemist. But at this point, there isn't much he can do. Now I have to swear I have a job for this kid and that he won't be a burden to the U.S. Government. Maybe I can train him to be a baker. You know they have a lotta formulas to worry about."

"It's a bit of a stretch," Rev. Turner said, laughing. "But maybe I can help." He paused for a moment, then folded up *The Morning Telegraph,* which was a signal that he was changing from his informal mode to one more in keeping with my father's immediate problem. "Our parish lawyer is an expert in this area."

"Just what I need," my father moaned. "Another lawyer!"

"Let me see what I can do," Rev. Turner said. "Marty O'Brien teaches a course in immigration law at Fordham Law School. If anybody knows how to help Lilly's nephew get out of Germany, Marty's our guy."

"But I bet he'll cost a fortune," my father said.

"He'll do it for me, Nate. He's our staff attorney."

"That's wonderful news, Les. Just to know that we may be able to do something to save this kid . . . well, Lilly will be very happy."

"I'm glad. I'll call Marty tonight, set everything up, and you can buzz him in the morning."

"Just one thing, Les," my father asked. "You say his name is O'Brien. Isn't that an Irish name?"

"Marty's as Irish as a shillelagh with a brogue to go with it." The reverend laughed. "Look, you want a smart lawyer in this town, you get a good Irish Catholic."

"Les, you're amazing," my father said. "Here you are—a big wheel in your church, yet you know the batting averages of the 1927 Yankees starting lineup and you're the best hearts player I ever came across. Isn't there anything you can't do?"

Rev. Turner laughed. "Stop eating your prune Danish, for one thing."

Just as he said that, there was a loud scream from the cellar. Freddie bounded up the wooden stairs, shouting, "Get an ambulance!"

Everyone—my mother and my aunts behind the sales counters, my father and Rev. Turner—ran toward Freddie. "Emil, the new guy, just collapsed at the worktable. He was makin' rolls—and then he just keeled over," Freddie explained breathlessly. "He's out cold."

"Oh, my God!" my mother screamed.

I thought it was odd that Freddie would refer to Emil as the "new guy." Emil had been working in the bakery for nearly two years but I guess, compared to the others, he could be considered new.

"Bertie!" my father yelled to my Aunt Bertha. "Call Fordham Hospital—get an ambulance!"

The only phone in the bakery was coin-operated. While my Aunt Bertha fumbled for some nickels in the cash register drawer, my father, Rev. Turner, Freddie and I all tried to squeeze down the narrow staircase leading to the cellar. My mother made an effort to stop me, but I quickly put myself between Freddie and Rev. Turner. I was almost 12 and had never seen a dead person before. I figured this was a chance not to be missed.

My father and Rev. Turner made it all the way down to the cellar. Freddie stood with me midway down the stairs. It was a grim, quiet scene.

The cellar was usually a frantic, noisy place. Mixers whirred constantly. Oven doors clanged sharply as they were opened and closed, as if punctuating the conversation and loud laughter from the bakers after one of them told a dirty joke.

But the only sound at that moment was the steady breathing of the stunned bakers crowded around poor Emil, who lay unmoving on the worktable. Only Uncle Menashe had stayed at his post at the oven to make certain that the last batch of Kaiser rolls did not turn into burnt rocks. I knew that it must have been hard for him to keep working because he was fond of Emil, whom he had trained personally.

"Is he alive?" my father asked.

"Yeah, but he don't look too good," Franz, one of the old-timers, said.

Suddenly, Emil started to mumble.

"He's Catholic, you know," said Otto, another baker. "He's gonna want the last rites."

"What's the last rights?" I whispered to Freddie.

"It's what they say when you're dying, so you can get to Heaven."

"An ambulance is on the way," my Aunt Bertha called from the top of the stairs.

"Are they sending a priest?" my father asked. "We need a priest."

"You shoulda told me, Nathan," my aunt grumbled. "I'm not a mind reader, you know."

Rev. Turner, who had been standing some distance from the table, moved forward. "I think I can help," he said confidently.

All of the bakers made room for the reverend. Otto, Franz and Walter, the baker's helper, quickly ceded their space to the man dressed in black.

"Oh, I didn't see you, Father," Otto said softly. Reverends, pastors, Fathers—they were all the same to Otto.

Rev. Turner leaned over the worktable and whispered into Emil's ear. Whatever he said caused Emil to lift his arm, motioning that he wanted to speak. This time, the reverend put his ear close to Emil's mouth, and Emil struggled to make himself understood. I doubt that anyone except Rev. Turner could hear him. The only words that traveled to my step on the stairs were "redemption from Jesus," which the reverend spoke softly and with great solemnity.

After a few minutes, the minister stood up straight and moved to the foot of the table. There he bowed deeply, as if he was a performer thanking an audience for their applause. But there was no applause, only the breathing of the bakers. Emil lay completely still.

Then, as if on a signal, everyone bowed their heads. At that moment, the Fordham Hospital ambulance crew arrived and we all scurried to get out of their way.

A few minutes later, we watched anxiously as Emil was brought up the stairs on a stretcher to the street level. I could see that his face had turned a sickly-looking gray color, his eyes were closed, and his mouth hung open, which emphasized the hollows of his cheeks. I wondered if this was what death looked like.

A few customers chatted softly with my mother and my aunts and the other salesclerks, but all activity upstairs had ceased.

As the crew was placing Emil into the ambulance, Rev. Turner spoke to the driver. "I'll go with him, if you don't mind," he said, climbing into the rear of the vehicle.

It was several minutes before the bakery returned to some semblance of normalcy. My Aunt Bertha, who had become the designated telephone operator, called Emil's wife and told her what had happened, assuring her that if Emil didn't make it, he would nevertheless be going to Heaven, since he had been given his last rites.

Freddie whispered to me that he didn't think it would really work, that only a Catholic priest could get someone into Heaven. I began to feel very sorry for Emil. Not only was he still considered, after nearly two years in my father's bakery, as a "new guy," but through no fault of his own he was likely to wind up in Hell.

Two hours later, just as we were getting ready to go home, a taxi
rolled up in front of the bakery and Rev. Turner stepped out. He
seemed fairly cheerful for someone who had just sent a man off to
his death without much hope of going to Heaven.

"He's going to be all right," he said excitedly. "It was a heart
attack . . . fortunately no damage . . . and with proper rest and care,
they say he'll be okay, although I don't think he'll be making challahs for a while. His wife, Margaret, got there just as he was coming
around. It was a lovely moment seeing them greet one another."

"Let me ask you something, Les," my father said. "How did you
know what to do with those Catholic prayers? They sounded pretty
official to me. All that Latin stuff."

Latin? I guess my father had heard more than I had.

"Well, my religious education was fairly broad," the minister
explained. "I can do a pretty good Passover seder if push comes to
shove, and even a Hebrew prayer for the dead." He winked at me.
And he started to recite, in Hebrew, the mourner's Kaddish:
"*Yisgadal, v'yiskadash sh'me rabbo . . .*"

"But don't get me started on that," he said. "Right now, I have to
call our Irish-Catholic friend, Marty O'Brien, and see if we can help
keep your German-Jewish nephew alive."

*Marty O'Brien did help with the paperwork that enabled 19-year-
old Josef Steinhardt to travel from Berlin to the Bronx. He worked in
my father's bakery for a little over a year, hating every moment of it.
For some reason that I was never privy to, he went to live in
Minnesota. He served in the U.S. Army during the war, earned a
degree in mechanical engineering and, with a brother-in-law, started a
successful tool and die business in St. Paul.*

*The only memento we have of his time in the Bronx is a copy of
Sinclair Lewis's* It Can't Happen Here, *which he gave to my sister
when she graduated high school in 1939.*

Amelia's Baby

After the death of my grandmother in 1933, my grandfather, Herschel, and my two bachelor uncles, Willie and Maxie, continued to live in the apartment on Bronx Park South where they had lived with my grandmother.

The apartment was quite unusual for its time and place. It consisted of six, large high-ceilinged rooms—easily 14 or 15 feet in height. The absence of any rugs on the gleaming, polished oak parquet floors made the spaces appear even larger than they really were. Best of all, from my point of view, there was a huge foyer that ran the length of the entire apartment, in which my cousin Jerry and I would play "catch" without fear of doing any damage to the walls or furniture.

I loved going there. When I was very young, it was also a great place for hide-and-seek, and there were always wonderful things to eat.

The main reason for the latter was Amelia Billingsley, who had been hired by my grandmother as a cook and housekeeper several years before the family moved from Yorkville to the Bronx.

When Amelia came to work for the family, she was barely out of her teens and had just recently arrived from Barbados. She was described to me by my mother as having been an extremely shy, withdrawn young woman. That changed as she became involved

with the lives of a family of energetic, opinionated men (my grandfather and my father) and confident and willful women (my grandmother, my mother, and her sisters).

When I first became aware of Amelia, she was a brisk, outgoing
woman—quite beautiful—with clear, dark-brown skin, which shone
like marble. There was also a bit of the flamboyant about her; she
dressed in brightly colored clothes that seemed to say, "Come, have
a look!"

From the outset, it was Amelia's job to take care of all of the
domestic chores in the apartment while everyone else went off to
work in the family bakery a few blocks away. She was a marvelously
accomplished individual. Every day, my grandmother would have
some perfunctory discussion with her as to what Amelia was to cook
for that evening's dinner, and that was it. Everything else was
Amelia's responsibility. From what I gathered, no one ever complained about the quality of her cooking.

My grandmother had spent just enough time with Amelia, in those
early years, to teach her the fundamentals of the German cuisine she
had brought with her from Berlin. Amelia must have added her own
West Indian touch to the meals served on Bronx Park South, because
I am sure the ginger and coconut chicken she prepared for us did not
come from the Hackescher Markt district of Berlin.

I have been told that my grandmother was an excellent cook but
preferred the environment of the retail bakery business to cooking
and apartment cleaning. She loved everything about the bakery, particularly the friendships she developed with many of the customers.
She reveled in the adulation and respect she received from the salesclerks whom she'd trained meticulously. She thrived on the attention
and devotion of the old-world bakers who catered to her as if she
was royalty. And, finally, she enjoyed the humor and conversation of
the wisecracking men whose real purpose was to sell flour and yeast
and egg yolks to my grandfather and my father. Who wanted to stay
home and cook and clean when they could have all of that? My
mother followed a similar path when it came to choosing between

housework and business.

After my grandmother died at age 60 from the ravages of diabetes, no one seemed to give much thought to whether Amelia would remain in her job. There was still my grandfather and my uncles, Maxie and Willie, to take care of, and who better to do this than Amelia? Maxie was quiet and undemanding, and Willie was out of the apartment most of the time. He was a fabled, one-armed athlete, an especially skilled basketball player, whose lackadaisical work habits drove my grandfather, and later my father, wild. Uncle Willie enjoyed a lively social life, which was limited entirely to men, most of whom were involved in sports. He showed no interest in women unless they could sink 25-foot set shots or were adept at a "zone defense."

So my grandfather went on with his life, which consisted mainly of working in the bakery ten or twelve hours a day. Occasionally, he would take an afternoon off, and go with Uncle Maxie to the Polo Grounds to see the Giants play even though he never really understood baseball. Evenings were spent in the back room of the bakery, where he played poker and pinochle with my father and their mutual friends, most of whom had their own bakeries in other parts of the city.

As she had done before my grandmother's death, Amelia came to the apartment every morning around ten and stayed until after dinner, usually about eight in the evening. She continued to take one day off during the week and Sunday mornings, when she went to church. She lived with a sister in the Mott Haven section of the Bronx, and traveled by trolley car to work. No one in our family seemed in the least interested in Amelia's life away from Bronx Park South. But that would change soon enough.

My mother had assumed my grandmother's role with regard to the overseeing of Amelia's work as housekeeper and cook. (It was felt that this was necessary because neither my grandfather nor either of his sons was interested in such domestic doings.) Once or twice a week, my mother would stop by the apartment on Bronx

Park South with a shopping bag loaded with baked goods, have a cup of coffee with Amelia and inquire about the domestic comforts of her father and brothers. Occasionally, I accompanied my mother on one of these "check-ups," as she called them. I was more than happy to go with her as it gave me an opportunity to get away from my homework for a little while, and I could always rely on Amelia to supply me with some delicacy as a reward for "helping" my mother.

"You think Amelia's got a chocolate pudding for me?" I asked as we walked the three blocks from the bakery to my grandfather's apartment building.

"Whatever she gives you, it'll be good," my mother said with a smile as we entered the lobby of the building and made our way into the elevator.

When we arrived at my grandfather's floor, the pungent odor of potted brisket of beef filled the entire hallway. "There's no doubt about it," my mother whispered, "that *schwarze* cooks like she was born on 82nd Street and First Avenue."

"Is that good?" I asked.

"Very good," my mother answered.

"Why do you always call her a *schwarze*?" I challenged my mother. "Isn't that insulting?"

"Not at all," my mother said. "*Schwarze* is just 'black' in German."

"But Amelia is brown," I countered.

My mother gave me a sharp look. She probably had more to say but by then we had come to the door of my grandfather's apartment.

From the moment she greeted us, I could tell that Amelia was not her usual, buoyant, loving self. There had never been a visit that I did not receive an all-enveloping hug and a wet kiss on my forehead. But this time, she handed me a small bowl of chocolate pudding and motioned me toward the swinging door that led to the dining room. "You go into the other room, young man, and eat some chocolate pudding," she said sternly. "Your mother and I have some things to talk about that are none of your business."

AMELIA'S BABY ✐ 73

My mother seemed as surprised as I was by my quick dismissal, but before she had a chance to say anything, Amelia had managed to push me gently into the dining room, and the swinging door was already shut.

I was a little put off by this, and I was not about to be bribed by some of Amelia's chocolate pudding. I planted myself as close to the door as possible, so as not to miss whatever Amelia had to talk to my mother about.

"Are you all right?" my mother asked.

"Oh, I'm fine, Lilly. It's just that I got myself into a real mess."

"A mess? You mean money? Look, that can happen to anyone, especially these days," my mother said. "Don't you—"

Amelia cut my mother off. "It ain't about money. Fact is, I'm pregnant. Gonna have a baby right after the New Year."

I could only imagine my mother's expression but I could actually *hear* her quick intake of breath.

"My God. How'd you do that?" my mother exclaimed.

Amelia laughed. "The usual way, Lilly. You know, with a man."

"This is not funny, Amelia. Is this man going to marry you? Is he prepared to support this baby?"

"I have no intention of marrying him," Amelia responded firmly. "And what's more, I can take care of this baby by myself. That's if it's okay with the family?"

"What do you mean, if it's okay with the family?" my mother asked. "You just tell me who the father is, and I'll make sure he takes care of you *and* the baby."

I didn't know what my mother had in mind by this. Maybe she would get some of Uncle Willie's basketball players to go after this guy? Or maybe my Uncle Phil could beat him up? He was a pretty strong guy.

"It don't matter who the father is. I don't want to marry him. And I don't want his money," Amelia said. "All I want is to be able to stay working for the family and take care of the baby—right here."

For a moment or two there were no more words for me to hear.

All I knew was that Amelia was crying.

"It's okay," my mother finally said. "It's okay. You can still work here and bring the baby with you every day."

Amelia sighed. "Thank God."

"Don't thank Him, thank me." My mother giggled. "I don't know what Poppa is going to think about all of this. He's going to want to know how this happened. He's going to want to know who the father is."

"It don't matter who the father is. Ain't nobody's business—especially your poppa's."

Again, there was silence. I felt nervous. What did Amelia mean by "especially your poppa's"? I wondered if my grandfather would be annoyed or angry about having a crying baby around the house.

Suddenly, the swinging door was pushed open; I just managed to get out of the way in time.

"Didn't you finish that wonderful chocolate pudding I made for you?" Amelia asked. "You haven't been listening to your momma and me talking, have you? You know it ain't right to listen in on other people's conversations. Especially grownups."

I couldn't think of a thing to say, so I started eating the chocolate pudding as fast as I could.

That evening, shortly after dinner, my aunts Sylvia and Bertha came to our apartment. They both wore serious expressions, so I guessed that my mother had already filled them in with the essentials about Amelia over the telephone.

"How in hell did she get pregnant?" my Aunt Sylvia asked.

"The way everyone does, silly," was her sister Bertha's response.

"Oh, you know what I mean! Really, she needs this like a hole in the head."

"Well, what I'm really feeling kind of funny about is the way she kept avoiding telling me who the father is," my mother said anxiously. "You know, I had a feeling like it was someone we might know, although I can't imagine who."

"I don't know if you're thinking what I'm thinking," Sylvia said quietly. "But you know, there's only men in that apartment—besides Amelia. Just Willie, Maxie and Poppa. With Momma gone and all."

"Well, you can forget about all of them," Bertha said defensively. "Maxie is . . . well, he may be my twin brother, but we all know he's a bit on the dumb side."

"Hey, it doesn't take brains," Sylvia said with a giggle.

"Girls, please. Get serious," my mother said.

"I *am* serious. Maxie could never . . . " Bertha insisted.

"And, as far as I know, Willie has never, *ever* looked at a woman!" my mother said.

"So, you think Poppa . . . ?" Sylvia asked.

Suddenly, my Aunt Bertha turned and saw that I was still in the room, pretending to be reading a book. "What the hell are you doing here?" she demanded. "Who invited you into this discussion?"

"Nobody. I was just . . ."

"You were just leaving, so leave. This is grownup stuff," Bertha continued.

"Oh, let him stay," Sylvia said. "He's old enough."

I really loved Aunt Sylvia. I could always count on her at times like this.

"No," my mother insisted. "He goes now. Go to your room—fast!"

I left without protest, but I was not about to be kept in the dark about this. I deliberately made some noise as I made my way to my room. Then I closed the door, making sure I remained on the outside. After a moment, I tiptoed back toward the living room, as close as I could get to the sound of their voices without being seen.

There were no words spoken for a few moments. I guessed they wanted to make sure I had indeed gone to my room. And then they started again, all at once.

"It can't be Poppa."

"Why not? He's not that old."

"Momma's been dead for six years."

"That's a long time for a man like Poppa to be without a woman."

"Amelia's a very attractive girl."

"She's always been fond of Poppa."

"Fond of someone is one thing, but . . ."

Then there was dead silence. I hustled back to my room. Alone, I also wondered if my grandfather could actually be the father of Amelia's baby.

Over the next few weeks there was little said or done that would shed any light on the mystery of Amelia's pregnancy. Uncle Willie laughed about it and said he couldn't wait to teach the baby—whom he assumed would be a boy—the fundamentals of basketball. Uncle Maxie didn't say anything, but that was more or less expected. My grandfather seemed genuinely surprised when he was told. His only comment was that it would be nice to have a new baby around the house again.

Weeks and then months went by. Amelia grew larger and, if it was possible, she was more effervescent than ever. Her Friday night dinners became weekly banquets. With Amelia so visibly pregnant, the grownups gave up on sending me out of the room whenever the conversation turned toward Amelia's baby. Accordingly, I can tell you that no matter how many times she was asked, Amelia would not discuss the identity of the father. As long as she could stay working for the family and could take care of her child, she would be happy.

But my mother and my aunts were not satisfied. They agreed that they would put the question: "Are you the father?" directly to Uncle Willie and Uncle Maxie. Both denied they had anything to do with it. Willie, in fact, was so angry that he did not speak to any of his sisters for several days. Uncle Maxie smiled. My Aunt Sylvia surmised that he was happy just to have been asked.

But of course none of the sisters had the courage to confront their father.

"We'll just have to wait and see what comes out," Sylvia said.

"Well, if the baby is very dark, that'll only prove it wasn't Poppa. But if it turns out to be a mixture—you know, a kind of light tan— it just proves that the father was white and it doesn't necessarily mean Poppa is the father. Right?" There was some logic to what my mother said.

New Year's Day, 1940, came and went, and with Amelia looking ready to give birth any day, my mother and my aunts became more anxious than ever. Then, one afternoon, my mother received a call at the bakery from a nurse at Sydenham Hospital on 125th Street in Harlem. Amelia had come to the hospital that morning, and there were complications around the delivery. She had asked, specifically, if my mother could come to the hospital.

By the time my mother arrived, so had a chubby, very dark, healthy, nine-pound baby boy—who was quickly named by Amelia: Herschel William Max Billingsley.

Herschel?

"Yes. Isn't that sweet?" A weary Amelia smiled up at my mother, explaining that her baby, Herschel William Max Billingsley, was "named after my three favorite men!"

When my mother told us about Amelia's newborn son, I couldn't tell if she was pleased that the baby had been named after my grandfather and my two uncles, but I was confident that she was relieved that the baby's "beautiful dark skin" erased any uncomfortable suspicions about who the father might be.

The family celebrated little Harry's arrival a few weeks later with a small party at the Bronx Park South apartment. (The name "Herschel" seemed a bit much for someone so tiny.)

A corner of Uncle Maxie's room was turned into a part-time nursery. Uncle Willie put a miniature basketball in the crib. My grandfather gave Amelia a check, the amount of which I didn't know, but which made Amelia cry with joy.

Not long after Amelia and her son had settled into a daily routine at my grandfather's apartment, my mother and my aunts began to

develop this notion, that, perhaps, it was time for their father to . . .
you know . . . maybe start looking for a wife? Maybe he needed his
own woman around the house? After all, it was almost seven years
. . . and Poppa was really not that old.

A Love Affair

I believe that there was a good deal of "hanky-panky" going on in my father's bakery. Not that this kind of carrying-on was peculiar to *his* shop; the fact is, it was common to all bakeries.

Think about it. Were butcher shops ever a place where romance flourished? Did the atmosphere of delicatessens or appetizing stores or greengrocers or dairies or fish markets encourage an interest in sex?

Bakeries had a great deal going for them in this department. As soon as you entered, there were the intoxicating aromas of breads baking and the luscious smell and look of creamy chocolate, glistening on rows of layer cakes. All of the senses were aroused, including the sexual.

And then, too, consider that the number of men and women working in the bakery was pretty evenly balanced: the bakers were all men and almost all the salesclerks were women. Do you see where I am going?

In addition, while most retail shops closed around dinnertime, bakeries remained open, usually until eleven o'clock, and even later on Friday and Saturday nights. And shortly after the retail business closed, the bakers arrived to start the next day's production. Who was there to see that they spent all of their time mixing flour and water and yeast?

Finally, there were a number of warm, cozy places in a bakery in which things could and, I am told, did happen. While I never actually witnessed anything, there was talk among the bakers, as they carefully kneaded a mound of soft dough, about how they would like to get Anna or Millie or some other female clerk in my father's bakery onto a pile of flour sacks.

One day, when I was in my early teens, and putting in some time at the worktables, Franz demonstrated how to knead two balls of dough at once. "You see, kid, watch how I do it. I roll each piece of dough in opposite directions, soft and easy," he whispered, as his large, coarse hands seemed to caress the pillow-shaped mounds of slowly rising dough. "You don't want to hurt them. Make believe they're a woman's breasts."

I was somewhat unnerved by the analogy but I apparently did well because Franz continued: "That's good. You must be doing okay with the ladies." And then he laughed.

As far as I know, the romance between my Aunt Sylvia and Mr. Schulman, my father's landlord, did not actually take place in the bakery itself, but it was there that the first sparks of their love affair developed.

My Aunt Sylvia was my favorite among my mother's sisters. My father was especially fond of her, too. He loved her free spirit and the way she laughed at all of his stories. He used to say that she would have been better off if she had been born into his side of the family rather than my mother's, which was more inclined to somber reflections than to celebrations.

Aunt Sylvia loved to have fun. She loved horse racing, gambling, singing, dancing and men. God, did she love men!

When my older sister, Edith, had been about twelve, she had heard the girls at school whispering about getting their periods. She had gone to my mother and asked her to explain about menstruation, sex, boys, etc. My mother had been horrified. "Go talk to your Aunt Sylvia," she'd advised. "She can tell you everything."

And my sister did, and my aunt cheerfully, and in great detail, told her everything any pre-teenage girl needed to know, and probably a great deal more.

Of course, I didn't hear about all that until later, but it fits in with everything I know about my Aunt Sylvia.

Aunt Sylvia had been married twice. Her first husband was a luckless chap named Arnold Freed. In the brief time that they were together, they managed to have one child, a daughter, Norma. But shortly after she was born, Arnold Freed succeeded in committing suicide by throwing himself off the roof of 1900 Vyse Avenue, the building where he had brought his new family to live.

I wasn't born until a few years later, but I gathered from the family's biased view that Aunt Sylvia's first husband had been a strange, moody individual. One minute he'd be fine, happy as a lark, chatting away, and then he'd clam up, never say a word for hours at a time. My mother said she never understood what Sylvia saw in him but, in those days, women were under enormous pressure to get married, and Arnold Freed was a butcher who made a good living. And, from the few photographs that remained in the family's albums through the years, I think he could have passed for Rudolph Valentino.

The first few months after Arnold Freed's suicide, Sylvia had a rough time. She was young, and her husband's sudden death had devastated her. My mother and my Aunt Bertha took her and the baby, Norma, to Lakewood, New Jersey, a popular resort town where she could be away from Vyse Avenue, which had become a constant reminder of Arnold's terrible death.

When they'd returned to the Bronx, Sylvia and her baby had gone to live in my grandfather's apartment. But that did not last long. As Sylvia put it: "The only men around are my pop and my two ugly brothers." She soon found a place of her own.

About six months after Freed's demise, she started to date. There was one guy that my Aunt Hannah from Brooklyn, my mother's oldest sister, fixed her up with—a man named Eddie Franks, whom she found particularly attractive. He was considered quite a catch because not only was he American-born he was also a college graduate and a lawyer.

They went to the racetrack, Broadway shows, dancing. All very romantic and expensive. Eddie was totally taken with my aunt, and she relished his extravagant style of courtship. The only problem was that while Eddie appeared to be madly in love with Sylvia, he was also insanely jealous of any man who dared to give her more than a passing glance.

My mother said, recalling this particular time in Sylvia's checkered love life, that it was a formula for trouble.

My aunt was, of course, a born flirt. No male escaped her charm. Old men, young men—it made no difference to Sylvia. For the most part, it was all in fun. But Eddie would go wild if she so much as looked at another man.

Everything came to a head on New Year's Eve, 1925. My parents and my aunts and uncles always went to a party in a club in Yorkville, in their old neighborhood. Sylvia was doing her usual number, greeting old friends, male and female, with hugs and kisses, and Eddie was getting more upset as the minutes ticked off the old year.

The band started to play and everyone began singing the words to the new hit song, "I'm Sitting on Top of the World." Before anyone could get to the words, "I'm quitting the blues of the world," Aunt Sylvia began leading a line of dancers, including my father and his two younger brothers, Ruby and Charley, in a wild dance, weaving around all the tables in the banquet hall. It was one of those let-it-all-hang-out moments that was so characteristic of my Aunt Sylvia. "I just phoned the Parson/Hey, Par, get ready to call./Just like Humpty Dumpty/I'm going to fall." Everyone loved it except, of course, Eddie, who switched from sipping Champagne to gulping Scotch whiskey.

Later that night, after Eddie brought Aunt Sylvia home to the new apartment she had rented on Mohegan Avenue, they started arguing. Eddie, who was probably feeling the effects of too much J&B, raised his hand as if he was going to hit her. My aunt, it should be noted, could argue and scream with the best of them—but hitting or punching was not for her. He never did strike her. But it was the end of Eddie.

Oh, he tried to see her, to apologize. He was extremely embarrassed. He even called my Aunt Hannah to see if she could intervene on his behalf. But Hannah knew her sister and told Eddie not to waste his time. He had crossed the line, and Sylvia was not about to take him back.

Later that week, when my mother came to help care for the baby for a couple of hours, Sylvia confessed that she'd known, from the beginning, that things were not going to work out with Eddie. She'd realized that, eventually, the combination of her need to be admired constantly by as many men as possible, and Eddie's obsessive jealousy, would lead to some sort of explosion. "So, it's better it all came out now before he got too involved with Norma," she told my mother as she smothered her fatherless child with warm, wet kisses.

Finding a father for Norma became my Aunt Sylvia's single-minded crusade. She would do almost anything to please a man who would love her baby. And that's where Mannie Fox entered the picture. Mannie and his brothers owned a couple of trucks, and they had a nice thing going in the furniture trade. They would bring up the pieces from the South and deliver them to the small factories that were scattered on the West Side and on the Lower East Side of Manhattan, as well as to several shops that operated in Yonkers, just north of the city. It was long hours and hard work but they made a good dollar.

A few months went by, and despite whatever doubts Sylvia might have had about Mannie—he could be incredibly dull—she decided that he was the best around. He was available and, most important, he adored little Norma. That was enough for Sylvia. She and Mannie were married in the very same hall that had been the scene of the New Year's Eve party that had led to Eddie's departure from her life.

Surprisingly, at least at the beginning of their marriage, Sylvia did manage to control her need for additional male attention. Her laughter and her joyousness were now centered on her two children—Betty, who had been born within a year after she and Mannie were married, and Norma, whom Mannie had adopted. And she had plenty of gaiety left over for her nieces and nephews, including me.

By then, the Great Depression was in full bloom, and the trucking business had gone *kerplunk* like almost everything else, so Sylvia went to work as a salesclerk in my father's bakery. My father loved having her there. If someone came in for some rolls, you could be sure that the customer walked out with the rolls and a half dozen Danish, too. She could somehow induce people—the women as well as the men—to spend more than they had intended. And they loved her for it! She always made them feel that it was okay to splurge now and then.

Sylvia's daily presence in the bakery not only pleased my father but, apparently, Danny Schulman as well. His fruit and vegetable store was, of course, only two doors away. And he was a real lady-killer. His movie-star good looks started with a perpetually tanned face that was all angles and ridges. He had long, muscular arms; whenever possible he wore the sleeves of his blue denim work shirt rolled up high to reveal not only his muscles but a series of exotic tattoos from his days in the Merchant Marine before the Great War. He was well aware of the effect he had on women.

By contrast, his wife, Margaret, was singularly unattractive—a squat, bow-legged woman with the face of an English bulldog. My father didn't seem to mind her appearance as much as he detested her nonstop complaining, which was on display whenever she came into his store to shop. "You call that a Danish? Don't try to sell me that burnt rye bread! Why don't you get wax-paper bags the way they have in the West Bronx?"

My mother disliked Mrs. Schulman because she would shop in a mink coat, even in April, just to let everyone know how rich she was.

One evening, after dinner, my father seemed grumpier than usual. I pretended to be continuing my homework at the kitchen table as he began having a whispered conversation with my mother, who'd been spending less time at the store than usual in recent weeks. My mother was at the sink, washing dishes. As the conversation went on, my parents became less cautious and their voices got loud enough for me to hear clearly what they were saying to each other.

" . . . every afternoon," my father said. "He comes in just when Sylvia is on her break."

"It just happens?"

"They have a cup of coffee together . . . "

"So, there's nothing wrong in that . . . "

"No, it's the way they look at each other."

"Like what?"

"Like you know what."

"Can't you be more specific than that?"

"There's the way she smiles at him."

"You don't really think . . . ?"

"I don't know what to think."

"If it's true, it's awful."

"And today, he reached across the table and touched her hand."

"And she didn't pull away?"

"Right in the store!"

"I don't like it."

The next week, my father reported that Izzie, his bookie, had seen Sylvia and Schulman at the track together.

"They should be more discreet about it," my mother moaned.

"Maybe you should talk to her."

"Talk to her? *You* talk to Schulman. *Then* I'll talk to Sylvia."

Schulman had a partner in his produce market, Dave Altchek, a quiet, hardworking fellow who rarely engaged in gossip or small talk. He lived with a widowed sister and her three children, whom he supported. Mr. Altchek excelled at hearts, one of the card games that were played around the large oak table in the back of my father's store. He was not someone you could have a grand time with, but he was considered a reliable person. So when he revealed the latest story about my aunt and Schulman, my father became further depressed.

"Schulman's wife knows what's going on," my father told my mother, after dinner. "Altchek said Schulman's wife threw him out. Schulman has already slept two nights on the cot in the back of their market. Can you imagine that?"

"Serves him right," my mother replied. A husband who strayed received no mercy from her.

"He goes to Altchek's place to take a bath and a shave."

"Altchek's sister must *love* that!"

"The affair heated up when they went to Saratoga last weekend."

"Sylvia and Schulman?"

"No. Sylvia and Mannie and Schulman and his wife!"

My mother was astonished. She dropped a dishcloth, and when she bent to pick it up, she knocked over a pitcher and two glasses—all of which hit the linoleum-covered floor hard enough to break. She was nearly crying by the time she found the broom and dustpan to clean up the broken glass.

When she was finished, she stood grim and speechless for a moment or two. "Where the hell did they get the money?" she finally asked.

"Whatta ya mean?"

"I mean, Mannie's business hasn't made a dollar in months. And they're spending weekends at Saratoga?"

"Schulman paid."

"Schulman paid? That's fine!" my mother screamed. She was so upset that she was beyond remembering that I was in the room. In a cruel, mocking tone that was new to me, she mimicked Schulman's voice: "Let's go away for a weekend to Saratoga. Your husband and my wife can watch the horses and you and I can fuck in the hotel room!"

I had never heard my mother utter the word *fuck* until then—and I never heard her say it again. (She died just before her 99th birthday.) I looked up momentarily from my book and then quickly left the kitchen.

The melodrama continued. Schulman's two sons entered the picture. They were both adults. One was a lawyer, and the other worked for the city, and they were both making good money. They came to my father with a proposition. They would give Sylvia $2,500 if she would end her relationship with their father. "It's a lot of money," my father told my mother. "They're very sincere. They love their mother and they see the way this is eating her up."

"Tell them to save their money. They'd be better off talking to their rotten father," my mother said, her voice rising with each syllable.

"They tried. Before they got very far, Schulman told them to mind their own business."

"Business? Committing adultery isn't a business," my mother shouted.

"I'll do something," my father said meekly.

The following Tuesday, his afternoon off from the bakery, instead of going to the track, my father took Sylvia to Dominick's restaurant. My aunt must have known it was important because they took a taxi there rather than the trolley.

According to my father, when he told Sylvia about what Schulman's sons had proposed, she turned white. All the blood drained from her face. And then she started to cry. Not just tears in the eyes but real sobs. Even the waiters at Dominick's took notice and stayed away.

My Aunt Sylvia's tears were for Schulman's sons, whom she kept calling "those poor boys." And because of them, she declared, "I will never so much as look at Danny Schulman again."

Aunt Sylvia also told my father to tell Schulman's sons that she wouldn't take their money, that they should take it and buy their mother a nice new mink coat because the rag she was wearing looked like shit!

All of this was discussed openly in my presence. I guess by then my mother and father were aware that I had a pretty good idea what was going on.

Soon the whole neighborhood knew what had happened. Schulman was angry and confused. He couldn't understand why Sylvia was doing this to him, and it was months before he spoke with either of his sons again.

I guess we all thought that that was the end of it. But then we heard that Mannie was upset that Sylvia had not taken the $2,500 from Schulman's sons.

"What woulda been the harm of taking the money? We coulda used it," he told my mother, who was busy dropping more glasses on the kitchen floor.

"I was only joking," he said quickly.

My mother did not think he was funny.

By this time, Aunt Sylvia, who was only in her late thirties and still a remarkably attractive woman, became, according to my mother, resigned to living out her life with Mannie. She told my mother that he was a good father, and that was still very important to her.

Some dozen years later, after World War II, when the trucking business picked up, she and Mannie moved to City Island, the Bronx's version of Nantucket. I think it was to get away from all the gossips. There were too many old ghosts haunting the neighborhood around 180th Street.

If Sylvia had become more subdued, particularly around men, she remained jolly Aunt Sylvia to her children and to her nieces and nephews. Who could resist a weekend at the seashore with Aunt Sylvia?

One night—it must have been around 1958 or so—at one of their all-ladies get-togethers, Sylvia confessed to my mother and my Aunt Bertha that she had never really ended her affair with Schulman— that they had continued to see one another and were still seeing each other. She had tried, she said, to keep her distance from him, but he was persistent. And they were really in love. They both had lousy marriages. But they had realized that if they wanted to continue to enjoy one another and not hurt everyone around them—especially their children—they would have to be discreet. No more afternoons at the track or weekends in Saratoga, for sure. They could no longer flaunt their relationship.

I never did get any more of the details. You know as much as I do.

When Schulman died a few years later, my parents and I went to the funeral, but Aunt Sylvia made a point of staying away. She did not want to embarrass Schulman's family. But his death was a real blow. I visited with her a few days after the funeral, and I thought she laughed too long and too loudly at a modest joke I told her. She was trying to put up a good front.

A few years later, Mannie developed lung cancer and died while he and Aunt Sylvia were visiting Norma, who was living in Florida. Aunt Sylvia no longer had a reason to keep the house on City Island, so she decided to move out to San Diego to be close to her younger daughter, Betty, who recently had made her a grandmother.

The night before Sylvia was to leave, she told my mother that the moments she and Schulman had together, the love they had for one another, made up for all the difficult times she had had in her life. Schulman, she told my mother, "made me feel like a woman."

The Price of Doing Business

My father called it "the price of doing business." Customers would threaten to bring a lawsuit against the bakery for something that might or might not have happened while they were on its premises, or from eating an apple pie or other baked goods that they had purchased. They could be very inventive.

Occasionally, a person would have a real case, but just as often it was a plot to extort some easy cash. Most of the shops along East 180th Street were subjected to this kind of harassment, but I think my father's bakery must have looked like a goldmine to these would-be plaintiffs.

It was hard to claim that a food item sold in the cheese and egg store next door was contaminated. Oh, a rotten egg might turn up now and then, but Charlie, the owner, would quickly admit a "candling error" and replace the offending culprit with a fresh, unblemished one or, perhaps, even two.

On occasion, an odd object might find its way into the belly of a mackerel from one of the two fish markets on the block—but I don't recall hearing of anything serious.

If someone found a worm inside an apple from Schulman's produce stalls, Schulman or his partner would offer a perfunctory apology and hand the mildly nauseous customer not one but several apples.

Once, the live chicken market, which was located directly opposite my father's bakery, was all aflutter because, instead of a stray feather, a woman said she found a bloodied suede glove inside her holiday capon. That caused more laughter than anguish and was quickly resolved by an extra helping of free chicken livers. Nobody ever did figure out where the suede glove came from, since none of the chicken pluckers was likely to own such a luxurious item.

The bakery was not always so lucky. No matter how scrupulous my father and the bakers were, objects other than flour, sugar, cocoa, eggs, cream, fruits, etc., managed, somehow, to find their way into a chocolate brownie or an apple crumb cake, or even a simple rye bread. The most common intruder was a sliver of wood from the worn side of a bread-proofing box or a wooden worktable. A sawdust chip might, inexplicably, wind up in a custard éclair. Once, the wedding ring from a newly married baker's helper landed in the crevice of one of the challahs that was about to enter the oven. Fortunately, Uncle Menashe spied it before it reached the 400^0 heat.

Another time, when I was at a rear table doing my homework, a woman stormed into the bakery and confronted my mother, claiming she had broken a tooth biting into a buffalo nickel that was resting under a piece of onion inside a Miami-style onion roll (these are the ones in which the onions are inside the pocket of the roll). My mother apologized profusely and offered to send her to our dentist, who had an office in one of the apartment houses up the street.

"You think you're gonna get off that easy?" the woman responded angrily. "When my-son-the-lawyer is through with you, we'll own this whole store!" She said "my-son-the-lawyer" as one word.

My mother, who was not easily intimidated—after all, she had already lived with my father for more than twenty years—responded calmly. "Look," she said, "I really feel sorry about your tooth . . . "

"Tooth? It's not just a tooth, it's a whole bridge!"

"Well, I'm sorry about your bridge," my mother continued, beginning to get an edge to her voice. "But I am offering to have it fixed by my dentist, and I am sure our insurance company will make some compensation for the pain you have suffered."

"There's gonna be a lot of compensation when my-son-the-lawyer gets through with you. You can't imagine what I went through. And I'm still in pain now!"

I could see that the woman's threats angered my mother. Her face seemed to harden, and I knew it was only a matter of seconds before her speech would become extremely precise as she moved into her cross-examining mode. She didn't listen to *Mr. Keen, Tracer of Lost Persons* or *Phillip Marlowe* on the radio for nothing. "Can I see the roll and the nickel?" she asked.

"Of course," the woman responded, no doubt beginning to savor the rewards that would soon be coming her way. She handed my mother a small white paper bag with the imprint of the bakery on it. Inside was a half-eaten onion roll and a buffalo nickel.

My mother looked carefully at the contents of the bag, and then she handed everything back to the woman. "Looks to me like a stale onion roll and a nickel," she purred.

"Are you saying I am a liar?" the woman screamed. "Wait'll my-son-the-lawyer hears about this!"

"What is he going to hear?" my mother asked evenly. "That you came in here saying you broke a tooth—no, a bridge—biting into a roll from my store, and that I offered to have my dentist fix your teeth and then see that our insurance company compensates you for any pain you might have suffered?" She smiled tightly. "That's what I said. Word for word."

The woman started to speak, then said nothing.

My mother continued, this time her voice turned up a few decibels. "But that's not good enough for you. You threaten to take away our business. So, here's your roll back—and your nickel. For all I know, it came right out of that purse you're carrying."

A few days later, a man in his mid-twenties came into the store and asked to speak with my mother, who was putting the final string around a box of butter cookies.

"Hello," he said. "I'm Eddie Aronson. My mother was in to see you a couple of days ago about a tooth she broke biting into a roll she bought here. Well . . ."

"Ah, yes," my mother interrupted, ready for whatever my-son-the-lawyer had in store for her. "I thought it was a whole bridge, not just a tooth."

"Well, it was a tooth—a large one, but I'm not here to sue you. Actually, I want to apologize and, if I may, I'd like to take you up on your offer to have your dentist fix my mother's tooth. We're not looking for anything beyond that. I think it was wrong for my mother to threaten you the way she did."

"She actually told you what she said?" my mother asked.

"Yes. And now she feels bad. Actually, it was some of the neighbors who put her up to it. My father's been out of work for months, and now that she's got a son who's a lawyer, she figured it's an easy way to make a dollar."

"Well, I appreciate what you are doing. We all feel terrible when anything like that happens, but sometimes it can't be helped, no matter how careful you are," my mother said as she fumbled though her pocketbook for a card with Dr. Fine's phone number. "But the worst part is that I thought we were going to lose a good customer. I've seen your mother in here many times before this happened. It seems to me she's been shopping here ever since we opened."

"You're probably right," Eddie Aronson said. "As long as I can remember, you've been our bakery." He smiled broadly. "Hey, I don't think I could have survived law school without your rye breads."

A few weeks later, Mrs. Aronson and her-son-the-lawyer, Eddie, stopped by the bakery—Mrs. Aronson to show off her new false tooth that Dr. Fine had inserted after removing the broken one, and Eddie to buy a well-seeded rye. They told us that the insurance company had offered to send Mrs. Aronson $100 for her pain and suffering, and that they were more than satisfied.

As the Aronsons were leaving, my mother handed the woman a box of butter cookies. "A little something extra to try that new tooth on," she said.

Not all of these potential lawsuits ended so amicably. Once, during a regular delivery of flour, an elderly woman came zooming down the metal delivery chute that was used by the Pillsbury company to deliver its flour to the bakery. The chute stretched from the Pillsbury truck, across the sidewalk, through the open bakery cellar door, to the cellar below.

The woman, who had been told repeatedly by the truck driver to walk around the vehicle and not try to step over the chute, had caught her shoe on it and slid down, head first, along with an 80-pound sack of Pillsbury's Best Winter Wheat Flour.

Perhaps she'd been in a hurry or hadn't liked the idea of walking in the street. In any case, she and the sack of flour arrived almost simultaneously, landing in the massive arms of Hans Bauer, one of my father's veteran bread bakers who, for a split second, didn't know what to grab first—the lady or the sack.

Her unexpected journey caused a great deal of commotion in the cellar. Eventually, the woman—Mrs. Mandelbaum, a longtime customer—was brought up to the store level by my father and Freddie. She was covered in flour, her hair in absolute disarray, and looked like something out of a *Katzenjammer* comic strip.

My mother and my Aunt Bertha rushed to help, and seated Mrs. Mandelbaum at a table near where I was doing my homework. "Are you sure you're all right?" my mother asked. "We can call for an ambulance."

"No, no," she insisted. "Mr. Mandelbaum would faint if I went to a hospital. Anyway, I'm perfectly fine. It was just such a shock. Please, all I want is for you to call my husband.

"We have our own telephone, you know," she added proudly. Then she looked a bit puzzled. "If I could only remember the number . . ."

"Bertha," my mother said, "Please make Mrs. Mandelbaum some

tea, and I'll look up the number."

"Just tell him I'm okay," Mrs. Mandelbaum said. "But he should come and get me."

About ten minutes later, a harried Mr. Mandelbaum arrived. The first thing he saw was the big red sign on the side of the delivery truck: "Pillsbury—The World's Largest Flour Merchants." So even before he got inside the store, the wheels must have started turning in his head.

"Don't worry about a thing," he said, as he ran toward his wife. "First thing we do when we get back home is call a lawyer."

Fortunately for my father, the lawsuit that came a few weeks later was directed primarily against "The World's Largest" rather than East 180th Street's finest.

My father did not even have to hire a lawyer. The manager of the local Pillsbury sales office said his company would handle everything. And it did, much to the Mandelbaums' satisfaction. The only one who seemed to suffer any extended damage was Hans, who'd been too frightened to work the chute at the next flour delivery.

There were other accidents that plagued the bakery.

Occasionally, an undetected housefly could make its way into a batch of dough. A fly, when baked in a roll or in a rye bread, resembles a raisin. How many of these creatures have been consumed mistakenly is a statistic I'd rather not contemplate. As far as I know, it was a rare occurrence, considering the hundreds of thousands of rolls and breads that passed through my father's bakery. Nevertheless, even one of these raisin/fly incidents is not a pleasant experience.

I can recall one such time in the spring of 1940.

I was at my usual homework post, listening to my father give advice to the Julie brothers, Max and Toby. They were old friends of his who recently had lost their own retail bakery to creditors. They were thinking about starting a new business, this time in New Jersey, as wholesalers, dealing mainly with restaurants. They were telling my father about a property they hoped to buy if they could get a loan from one of the brokerage firms that handled bakeries. My father thought it was a bad idea.

"You're not gonna be happy selling wholesale," he said. "There's no fun in that. You guys need to be around people."

"Aren't restaurants people?" Max asked.

"It's not the same. I seen you schmoozing with your customers, with the salesclerks. Nobody does it better. And anyway, you're gonna be up to your ears with the Teamsters Union."

"Hey, I can dance with a teamster if I have to," Toby said with a laugh.

Nothing seemed to faze the Julie brothers: neither the loss of their bakery on Freeman Street nor the prospect of having to move to New Jersey and deal with truck drivers instead of female customers and salesclerks.

Their conversation, which had been a half-idling one (they had actually come early to my father's bakery for their regular card game), was interrupted by two women who wanted to speak with my father. One woman was clutching a wrinkled, No.6 paper bag. There was something in the way she carried the bag—even I could sense that it held trouble.

The other woman addressed my father. "We have a complaint," she announced. "Yesterday we bought six rolls, and when my sister bit into one of them, she realized that she had bitten into a *horsefly*."

"That's terrible!" my father said. "I hope she didn't swallow it?"

"No, she didn't swallow the whole thing, but while she was chewing she noticed only half of it still in the roll."

The silent woman clutching the bag looked as if she was going to become sick all over again.

Suddenly, Max Julie jumped up from his seat. He pointed to the bag. "Here, lemme see that roll," he demanded.

"Who are you?" the frightened woman asked.

"I'm from the Board of Health," Max replied, sounding quite

official. "It just so happens that I'm in here checking out this bakery today. So far, they look pretty clean to me."

The woman handed the bag to Mr. Julie. He removed the offending roll, looked at it for a moment and then showed it to my father and me.

It was clear that it was a fly—one of those big, fat horseflies. Ugh! I thought I would vomit. Even my father turned away.

"It's obvious," Mr. Julie said. "It's just a big raisin." At which point, he broke off the piece of the roll containing the fly, plopped it into his mouth, took two quick chews and swallowed. "I love raisins," he said with a giggle.

Both my father and I were stunned by Max Julie's daring performance. The two women were flabbergasted.

"You ate the fly!" shouted the woman who was the spokesperson. "You've eaten the evidence!"

"I ate a raisin, lady," Mr. Julie said.

The woman who had bitten into the horsefly began to cry.

"This is awful. It's terrible," my father said.

What exactly was said next was lost in the confusion of crying and yelling. I can only remember that, through it all, the Julie brothers were grinning from ear to ear.

As the two women started to leave, my father ran to the bread counter. Quickly, he tossed a half dozen rolls into a bag, and then he added a rye bread; for good measure, he threw in six bagels. He caught up with the two distraught women at the door. "I'm sorry," he said, handing them the large bag.

After they left, he turned to the Julie brothers. "Jeezus. How the hell could you do that? That was disgusting! And you mighta cost me a customer!"

"Is that the thanks I get?" Max Julie grinned. "I figured I saved you from a lawsuit."

Even my father laughed at that. "Now you see why a wholesale bakery is not for you and Toby," he said. "Every day in a retail business there are hundreds of customers to deal with—and that's what makes it such fun."

A few days later, I noticed that one of the sisters—the shy one who had actually eaten half of the horsefly—was at the bread counter. She bought a rye bread, without seeds, and asked that it be sliced. She was taking no chances.

Hawk

Just about everyone outside the family called my Uncle Willie "Hawk" simply because he looked like one. He had large, almost sinister, dark eyes, which slanted down toward a long, hooked nose that was like the beak of a predatory falcon. High cheekbones added to this hawk-like appearance. In other respects, though, he was like a dove.

He had a way of relating to children and other underdogs that was unthreatening and sympathetic. He was so childlike himself, and I was so comfortable with him, that I was often inclined to call him "Unk," which he seemed to enjoy.

Uncle Willie was my grandmother's final effort at childbirth. He weighed more than thirteen pounds when he entered this world, dragging along a withered (or, perhaps, more accurately, a crushed) left arm that somehow grew almost to the length of his good right arm but was devoid of any strength. As a kid, I thought it looked like a bird's wing. There—still another avian-like feature.

I was always fascinated by Uncle Willie's withered arm. He kept it tucked into the pocket of a sweater or a jacket that, in one form or another, was always part of his wardrobe, winter or summer. He could do amazing things with his right arm, the good one. I marveled at the way he would tie his shoelaces, using a combination of very strong teeth and the agile fingers of his right hand to complete the intricate maneuver.

As a child, he was of great concern to his parents, especially my grandmother, who dragged him to a series of doctors, all of whom said there was nothing they could do to help him. At one point, she took her eldest daughter, my Aunt Hannah, and the baby, Willie, to Germany where the practitioners of medicine were considered superior even to the specialists at New York's own Lenox Hill Hospital. She was hoping for a miracle, but none was forthcoming.

So Uncle Willie grew up the pampered and adored little brother of four sisters and a guilt-ridden mother who unreasonably blamed herself for his deformity. The girls, my mother among them, took turns playing with him. They rolled balls in his direction and, with his one good arm, he rolled the balls back. Later, they bounced balls toward him, and he bounced them back. His good arm became a powerful instrument. By the time he was 12 years old, he was a head taller than most of his friends, and he could throw a baseball faster and farther than any of them. His sisters were no longer needed as playmates, and, frankly, the strength and speed generated by his good arm frightened them.

The game he most enjoyed and at which he was most skilled was not baseball but, rather, basketball, which came to dominate his life. It proved to be a game that a person with one good arm could play as well as, if not better than, most people blessed with two. It was also a game that was played all year long. In the summertime, when the heat in the gymnasiums became unbearable, the concrete schoolyard was always there. And it took only one arm to fling a ball into a basket.

But more than that, it was a game even a mother could love: nobody got hurt if a basketball hit you in the head, and no legs were broken if you were bumped from behind.

This was a time when the two-handed set-shot was the norm. People were amazed that Uncle Willie, with only one arm, could score from virtually anywhere on the court with such regularity. The fact is, his one good arm was so powerful that he could throw a basketball the length of the court with the speed and accuracy of a pitcher hurling a baseball.

By the time he was ready to enter high school, he was over six feet tall and a legend in the after-school gymnasiums. The basketball coach at the local high schools in the Bronx were salivating at the thought of getting the Hawk to play on his school's basketball team. There was only one problem: Hawk had other ideas. Once finished with the tenth grade, he vowed he would never ever open a book unless it was a telephone book. Books, as far as my uncle was concerned, were what you put under a kid when he was too small to see over the top of a kitchen table. And besides, if he didn't go to school, he could play basketball all day long.

Nobody really questioned his decision. My grandmother was happy if he was happy, and how could she get angry with a boy who had only one good arm?

So Uncle Willie's life was spent honing his basketball skills. He hooked on to countless amateur and semi-pro teams, playing games as far away as Wilkes-Barre, Pennsylvania, and Springfield, Massachusetts, the so-called birthplace of basketball. If he never made any real money, that was okay, too. He always had a room in my grandparents' apartment, and three squares a day.

When my cousin Jerry and I were old enough, Uncle Willie spent a great deal of time teaching us the finer points of the game. We were taught how to box-out an opponent, the proper execution of a jump ball, how to inbound, the backdoor, the give-and-go and, most important of all, we were counseled when and when *not* to shoot. He was a marvelous teacher: patient, encouraging, clear when demonstrating a particular move, and knowing just when we had absorbed all we could that day. He also treated us to chocolate ice cream sodas, whether we had done well or poorly.

A number of our friends, who were also tutored by Uncle Willie—Hawk, to them—went on to star on their high school and college teams. The coach at Evander Childs High School told me he appreciated my enthusiasm and my knowledge of the game but that I was too short to be anything except a guard, and unfortunately I lacked the speed for that position. I got over that rejection quickly when I was selected to write about sports, including basketball, for the school newspaper, *The Evander News*. That seemed to satisfy even Uncle Willie, who would often come to the games I was covering and point out to me certain aspects of the game that would find their way into my published accounts.

Just before the United States entered World War II, Uncle Willie finagled my father into investing in a professional basketball league. My father hated basketball, but how could he turn down a boy with only one good arm and a face that resembled a hawk? Anyway, it wasn't a helluva lot of money.

The teams were from the area. The one Uncle Willie wanted my father to invest in was the Jersey City Jewels, not to be confused with the legendary and highly successful Brooklyn Jewels. The arenas were really just gymnasiums. Some of my uncle's players were kids who had learned the game from him in the schoolyard at P.S. 67 on Honeywell Avenue and then went on to play at City College, Long Island University or Brooklyn College. Some of the other teams in the league boasted Hawk alumni as well.

One night we all traipsed out to Jersey City to see Uncle Willie's team (he was the Jewels' coach as well as its part owner) play its first game against the team from Trenton. It was not easy getting out to Jersey City in those days, so fifteen or sixteen members of my family, including my father, the team's reluctant investor, crammed onto a rented bus with the nine members of the Jersey City Jewels and their friends and relatives, including several players' wives or fiancées. There were also three young women whom I was told were girlfriends of the players. The girlfriends were carrying blue and gold pennants—blue and gold were the colors of the Jewels—and were going to serve as the team's cheerleaders.

My cousin Jerry and I thought the idea of cheerleaders was exciting and made the event seem important, like the college games at Madison Square Garden. Uncle Willie was a purist and hated the whole concept of girls with pompoms jumping up and down, and he did not speak a word from the time the bus picked us up in the Bronx until we arrived at the CYO (Catholic Youth Organization) Gymnasium in Jersey City.

Jerry and I sat on the team bench with Uncle Willie. Our job was to hand towels to the players as they came off the court during a timeout. But our greatest fascination was watching our uncle as he played the role of coach. He showed the same combination of determination and gentleness with this group of former college athletes as he did when he was tutoring a couple of 12 year-olds in a school gym: "You're hurrying your shot . . . remember you're not alone on the court . . . if you don't have the ball it doesn't mean you stand still . . . you're here to play, not to watch the game . . . keep your hand in his face . . . it's okay to set a pick now and then . . . if you're tired, let me know . . . we're all in this together."

Unfortunately, in spite of Uncle Willie's astute coaching, everything that could have gone wrong that night *did*. The public address announcer introduced the home team as the "Jersey City Jews," which angered almost everyone except the Jewels' starting center, Terry Kinsella, a redheaded Irishman my uncle had discovered some years back in the schoolyard of P.S. 67. Terry put a towel over his head like a prayer shawl and pretended he was praying.

Then, five minutes into the game, one of the refs became ill and vomited under the visitors' basket. It took forever to clean it up but the awful smell lingered even longer.

The lights kept dimming until finally, early in the second half, they went out entirely. When the lights were restored fifteen minutes later, half the crowd had left, and more important, half the players on both teams were also gone.

Later, there was a great deal of confusion as to how many tickets actually had been sold and how many had been given away as comps. My father, of course, was furious, and wanted to kill Uncle

Willie—one arm or no arms. My mother tried to put a perspective on things. She said that clearly basketball was such a gentle game that it could never become a professional sport, and that maybe it was best to leave it as a diversion for college boys.

Uncle Willie went back to playing in the schoolyard. He began working a few days each week in the bakery for my father, who simply could not stay angry with a boy with only one good arm. Mostly, Uncle Willie helped Freddie keep the shelves in the cellar of the bakery in some semblance of order. Nothing fazed Hawk—80-pound sacks of flour or 20-quart cans of egg yolks were moved about effortlessly. He occasionally worked behind the counter at night, filling in for an indisposed Uncle Phil.

Still, most of Uncle Willie's days and nights were spent playing and teaching basketball. Friends of mine have told me that they thought he worked for the school system or was an employee of the Parks Department. He taught them and, as time went by, he taught their kids as well. There was never a person who had in some way interacted with my uncle who was not associated with basketball. He was always included in the wedding parties of his "guys," and dutifully attended the bar mitzvahs, bat mitzvahs and confirmations of their children. But it all started with a ball and a basket. And he never ran out of new pupils.

When my own two girls were old enough, I put up a hoop in our suburban backyard, and Uncle Willie came out and demonstrated his one-handed foul shot. Into his sixties, he still had that soft touch and that wonderfully accurate one good arm. He treated my eight- and six-year-old daughters with the same care and knowledge that he'd expended on hundreds of eager boys from earlier generations. But I knew that when my daughters grew older and they no longer were little girls, my uncle's comfort level with them would drop substantially. And I wondered about my uncle's narrow, single-minded life. How much of it had he chosen for himself? Or had it, in part, been imposed on him?

Back in the Bronx, where Uncle Willie continued to live and teach the intricacies of basketball, change had also come. The Sugarmans and the Goldsteins became the Velezes and the Garcias. But the comments that could be heard on the concrete basketball courts were altered only slightly:

"Who the hell is this old man with one arm and the hawk-like face?"

"Hey, don't knock him, Jose. Did you see him sink that shot from mid-court?"

"Yo, I went one-on-one with him, and he faked me outta my sneakers!"

"Hey, Hawk, wanna teach my kid to shoot?"

One night, at a family gathering, Uncle Willie showed up wearing his usual sweater with buttons down the front, and the pocket into which he had tucked his withered arm. He looked different since I had last seen him. He confessed that he was suffering from the "family disease," adult-onset diabetes. He couldn't lay off sweets—the éclairs and the brownies—even though he knew that they were killing him. I tried to talk some sense into him but he was so used to doing what he wanted that there was nothing I could say that would change his way of life.

Six months later, I got a call from Sy Sugarman, one of the old Jersey City Jewels, who was then a senior partner in the second largest accounting firm in the city. He wanted to know what was up with Hawk. Nobody had seen him in months, and they wanted to have a reunion of all the guys from the old neighborhood, guys he had taught to play the game of basketball. I told him what I knew: Hawk's diabetes had gotten so bad that the doctors had been forced to amputate his toes. I told him that Hawk was confined to a wheelchair and was living in a nursing home in the still leafy section of the Bronx known as Riverdale.

The news was apparently too much for Sugarman. There was only silence on the other end of the phone.

"Sy!" I yelled. Again, no response. "Seymour—Sugarman, are you there?"

"Yeah, it's just so sad," he muttered.

"I know, but the fact is, he never took care of himself," I said, as some sort of explanation. "But it's a good place, and he seems happy. He's organized a staff basketball team. He says they have some great talent. All they need is to learn the nuances of the game."

Then I gave him Hawk's phone number and the address of the nursing home.

"Thanks," he said. "It's so sad he never was able to make a go of it in pro basketball."

"Maybe he was just a little ahead of his time," I said.

"Nah, that's not what I'm talking about," he said with great passion. "Maybe if that fuckin' referee hadn't gotten sick, and if the goddamn lights hadn't gone out, we might've started something— and Hawk would have made something of his life."

"But he did," I said.

The Magician

I have always been fascinated by magic tricks—not the really spectacular stuff you see on television and occasionally on the Broadway stage but rather the simpler, straightforward kind that begins with a guy with a pencil-thin mustache and a shiny tux saying: "Take a card, any card!"

Nowadays, that brand of magic usually involves some smart-ass kid or an uncle trying to liven up a family gathering. But there was a time when "take any card" magicians, particularly during vaudeville's heyday in the '20s, performed regularly on all of the theater circuits across the country.

My friend Ozzie's father, Alexander Petrie, had been one of these entertainers. He didn't actually start out that way. He had trained as an engineer in Budapest before emigrating to America. But while he was waiting for New York State to recognize his Hungarian credentials, he decided to put his hobby of doing magic tricks to work. He earned a modest living performing in the movie houses in the Bronx where the principal attractions were the silent films of Buster Keaton, Mary Pickford and Clara Bow.

As luck would have it, in 1924 he was spotted by a representative of a big time producer who put him on a bill with Will Rogers that toured the major vaudeville houses across the country. With a new career, he gave himself a more challenging name. He deemed himself: "Alexander the Great." And he never looked back. His engineering books were replaced by *Weekly Variety*.

This turned out fine until talking pictures, radio and the Great Depression combined to kill vaudeville altogether. For a while, he left Ozzie and his mother in their apartment on the Grand Concourse while he performed on cruise ships. By 1939, the war in Europe had begun, and the ocean liners became arms-bearing cargo ships or, worse, were turned into scrap iron. The venues for professional magicians had simply gone up in a puff of smoke. Alexander the Great had run out of luck.

Mr. Petrie became a cab driver. Unfortunately, in 1940, taxi riders were as rare as African orchids, so the Petries struggled mightily. They moved from the Concourse to a dreary fifth floor walk-up off Bryant Avenue next to the elevated trains that roared along Boston Road. Ozzie was enrolled in P.S. 6 on Tremont Avenue, and that is where we met and became good friends.

Sometimes, after school, Ozzie would come with me to the bakery where we would both sit and enjoy a snack of milk and whatever looked tempting in the way of chocolate cakes. On one of these visits, I thought it would be fun to give Ozzie a tour of the cellar where the baking was done. I knew that my father would not object, because we often had groups of kids from the local elementary schools come on what were termed "field trips." The Bronx Zoo, the Bronx Botanical Gardens and my father's bakery were regular stops on these school excursions.

We found Uncle Menashe busy placing a dozen unbaked challahs into the center part of an oven. "Watch me," he said, deftly sliding the head of his long-handled peel—a baker's wood paddle—out from under the braided loaves of dough. The loaves barely had moved, but now, instead of sitting on the broad, flat head of the peel, they were sitting on the very hot bricks of the oven.

"See, it's like magic." Uncle Menashe laughed. "You ever see how a magician slips a cloth from under a table full of dishes? That's what I do—maybe a hundred times a day." This was also part of Uncle Menashe's spiel to the schoolchildren on visits. Baking, he would say, is like magic. "You take a little flour and water and yeast, and soon you have a big mound of dough. You shape it, maybe decorate it with a few poppy seeds, and then you slide it into an oven. In no time, the sack of flour is a hundred rye breads or delicious challahs. Now, isn't that magic?"

It was Uncle Menashe's little speech that prompted Ozzie to reveal that his father had been a professional magician. A real magician! I couldn't wait to meet him.

Mr. Petrie was just as eager to meet me—or any of Ozzie's friends. Although he drove a cab from four in the afternoon, ending at four the next morning, he was never too tired to perform magic. The problem was, he needed an audience. So Ozzie and I filled that role. These magical interludes never failed to excite me.

"You must understand, kid," Mr. Petrie would say as he fondled a deck of tarot cards, "a magic show is not just the trick, it's all the things that protect and enhance the illusion."

I noticed that when he spoke as a magician, his voice deepened and was quite different from his regular soft speech. It resonated and rose and fell with each new phrase. When he was coming near the climax of a trick, it boomed, and I thought I could hear one of his prop skeleton bones rattling.

The walls of the Petrie apartment on Bryant Avenue were decorated with posters from some of the vaudeville theaters where Mr. Petrie had once performed. His favorite was from the Palace Theater in Manhattan. It featured Belle Baker who, the poster revealed, would be singing her new smash hit, "Blue Skies." It didn't matter that Belle was listed in bold letters, eight inches high, and Alexander The Great was barely visible; Mr. Petrie loved that poster. When he was in a particularly happy mood, he would sing in his rich performer's voice: "Blue skies, smilin' at me/Nothin' but blue skies do I see."

Other people in Mr. Petrie's circumstances might have seen thunderclouds, but Alexander the Great was not just a survivor, he was an optimistic one. When he performed a "coin through the handkerchief" for Ozzie and me in the grim, crowded room on Bryant Avenue, it was as if he were on stage at the splendid Erlinger Theater in Philadelphia, a 30-foot brocade curtain behind him, a powerful white spotlight beaming on his floor-length crimson cape—while two thousand eyes were riveted on a beautiful female assistant who was about to disappear in a puff of orange-colored smoke.

Ozzie's mother, who once had served, I was told, as his "beautiful assistant," was a tiny, moon-faced woman who perpetually looked as if she were about to cry. My mother, who kept mental tabs on the buying habits of her customers, figured out after just a few of Mrs. Petrie's visits that the taxi business was not doing too well. She never bought a coffee ring or a crumb cake. It was strictly a few rolls and, now and then, a whole-wheat loaf. So, if my mother knew in advance that I was going to Ozzie's apartment, she made sure I went there with a box of cookies and, if it was a Friday, one of Uncle Menashe's challahs.

One day, while Mrs. Petrie was visiting her parents in Brooklyn, Mr. Petrie showed us a letter he had received that morning from the American Society of Master Magicians or a similar-sounding organization. It proclaimed that Alexander the Great was one of a half dozen professional magicians who were to be honored for their contributions to the magic arts. It was like being admitted into the Hall of Fame of Magicians. Mr. Petrie was absolutely ecstatic. His face took on a rosy hue, and the heavy, dark bags that usually hung like wilted flowers under his eyes suddenly seemed to vanish, giving his face a firm, determined appearance.

"We have to go." He spoke in his best performer voice. "Who knows? Maybe it's a way to get back into the business." He hugged Ozzie, and then he turned to me. "You'll come, too. It should be fun."

And then he looked more carefully at the letter. "Christ," he murmured. "It's on a Sunday. I'll lose at least a half day's business."

He thought for a moment. "Ah, what the hell, there's plenty of Sundays but only one like this." Then he danced around the room, grabbed hold of four large silver rings and tapped them deftly until they were all connected. "How often does the world get the chance to honor Alexander the Great?"

The ceremony was to take place from one until four in the afternoon in Central Park. Ozzie and I were assigned to each carry one of Mr. Petrie's prop cases, badly scratched and wrinkled leather bags with the words "Alexander the Great" splashed across the sides—much like the lettering for our favorite comic strip, *Superman*. It was hard work dragging them to Manhattan, particularly when we had to climb up the subway stairs. But we made it into the park area, which was decorated with balloons and banners for the occasion.

On a small stage set up under two large shade trees, was a six-piece brass band huffing and puffing its way through "Pennies from Heaven." Sixty or seventy chairs were lined up in front of the stage. Along the edges of the seating area, a number of magicians had set up their tables and boxes and were performing or, as the case might be, bungling various tricks. One young Houdini was desperately trying to do a basic "short card" trick, which was one of Mr. Petrie's least impressive accomplishments. When the struggling magician failed the first time, he simply tried to do it again.

This was a no-no as far as Mr. Petrie was concerned. "Never do a trick a second time for the same audience," he had warned Ozzie and me. "When you do it a second or a third time, the spectators' chance of seeing the sleight-of-hand involved is increased many times over."

Suddenly, over the sounds of the brass band, and the laughing and clapping of the crowds watching the young magicians, we heard someone yelling from behind us: "Alex, Alex Petrie, you old goat!" We all turned to see a tall, handsome, gray-haired man, dressed in a circus barker's costume, waving his arms frantically.

"It's really you," he said, wrapping two powerful arms around Mr. Petrie, who appeared stunned and happy at the same time. "I'm so glad you could make it!" the man shouted. "We had a lot of trouble figuring out where you lived after you left the business."

While the two men hugged and kissed, Mrs. Petrie, Ozzie and I stood by, not quite sure what we should do. Finally, Mrs. Petrie interrupted the reunion. "Enough already, Herman," she said to the other man. "Save a kiss for me." Herman paused for a moment, and then beamed his smile at Mrs. Petrie.

"Am I crazy?" he asked. "I could be kissing this beautiful angel. Instead, I am wasting all my energies on this gorilla." He grabbed Mrs. Petrie and began kissing her with mock passion.

I learned then that Herman had been one of Mr. Petrie's mentors when he was just breaking into the business in the early '20s.

As the afternoon wore on, many in the crowd came over to greet Mr. Petrie. With each new visitor, he would pause and make a big fuss about introducing Ozzie and me. Of course, they already knew Mrs. Petrie.

I listened in awe as these old magicians recalled every show or trick they had ever performed . . . the awful hotel they had to stay in during a split-week in Milwaukee . . . the dog act who was not only cheating on his wife but also on his mistress and his assistant and his agent's wife. Some of the show business talk was like a foreign language, but I was fascinated with whatever I could understand.

One thing was clear. All these men had drifted away from magic as a profession. One was an accountant; another was in the garment business with his father-in-law; a third had become a successful (or so he boasted) owner of several midtown restaurants. Most tried to give the impression that they were glad vaudeville was behind them. It was so much better selling pots and pans or fitting eyeglasses. Mrs. Petrie told Ozzie and me that they were all liars. The only thing that was true was that none of them had been aware that Alexander the Great was now driving a taxi. That astonished them.

Before we knew it, Mr. Petrie and five other men were asked to come up on the stage to receive their awards. There was a flurry of music from the brass band: "Ain't She Sweet" was their marching music, followed by "Yessir, That's My Baby" as the sitting-down music.

Herman took the stage and introduced the president of the organization, a rather aristocratic-looking fellow dressed in white tails and a white silk top hat.

"Watch carefully now," Mrs. Petrie warned. "Things can get pretty wild from here on."

I tried to concentrate on what the speaker was saying but it was almost impossible: as soon as he started talking, the six honorees stood up and began performing a series of tricks. Rabbits were plucked from boxes that moments earlier clearly had been empty; pigeons emerged from brightly-colored silk scarves; decks of cards were stretched and folded like accordions; ropes were cut and then joined together again; glasses were filled with water—then they vanished in a cloud of blue-colored smoke.

Through all of this, I managed to catch a phrase or two from the apparently unfazed, upstaged speaker: "We must continue to pursue . . . in the face of difficult . . . I am happy to report . . . a bright future . . . their accomplishments will . . . and so I thank you . . . "

(I found out later that it was a tradition of the Society of Magicians that no one ever listened to the speech of the president. I still don't know why this was the case but it certainly was fun.)

Finally, it was time for the honorees to be recognized and the awards given out. Each of them was called to the center of the small stage and presented with a framed certificate. They each made a brief speech filled with curse words and outrageous comments about Herman and the president of the Society. (This, too, was a Society tradition.)

The last to be honored was Alexander the Great. He stood there for a few moments while the crowd of old colleagues and friends cheered and applauded. Finally, when he spoke, his voice resonated above all the mumblings of the crowd and the din of the street noises drifting into the park.

"I want to thank God for making me a magician," he said with gravity. "He could have made me a Rockefeller. He could have made me the King of England or J.P. Morgan. Maybe even Clark Gable or Jack Dempsey. He could have made me into a brilliant scientist or a great inventor like Edison. But he made me into a humble magician—and that's all I ever will be or want to be."

For a few seconds the crowd was silent, and then they erupted into loud and sustained cheering. Mrs. Petrie no longer looked as if she had just finished crying or was about to cry. She was weeping full blast.

It took several minutes before some order could return to the stage.

The magic-show finale surprised me most. A heavyset, bearded man in his 50s, wearing a yarmulke, walked onto the stage accompanied by a little girl who looked to be about eight or nine years old. The man introduced himself as Rabbi Mordecai Abrams. He explained he had been a professional magician before going into what he called the "family business." That brought a chuckle from the crowd. "Fortunately," he went on, "my daughter, Ruthie, is prepared to carry on the family vocation: magic. And today she is ready to show you a trick or two."

At her father's command, the little girl entered one of two, large closet-like cabinets that had been placed at either end of the stage. Before her father closed the door of the cabinet, Ruthie smiled and waved to the audience. After a few moments of conversation between the father and daughter, she asked to be let out. When her father opened the door, she was not there. Instead, she emerged from the second box at the other end of the stage. Once out, she closed the door quickly behind her and bowed with great flair.

The crowd applauded wildly, then quieted a bit. Suddenly, we all heard another voice yelling out from the box the little girl had just left.

Several people in the crowd screamed: "Let her out! Let her out!"

Feigning exasperation, the father opened the door, and probably to no one's surprise except mine, the box was empty.

Now, a shout came from the first box: "Let me out! Let me out!"

The father walked slowly over to the first box and—with a look of great doubt on his face—opened its door. A smiling Ruthie stepped out and quickly joined hands with her father and . . . her twin sister.

The crowd cheered. The show ended, leaving me dumbstruck.

Making my way through the dispersing crowd, I saw Mr. Petrie talking to the rabbi-magician while his little daughters stood nearby. Each girl had two hand puppets who were engaged in an animated conversation about school and ice cream with each other and their manipulators. The trick had involved not only twins but *ventriloquist* twins.

Meanwhile, the rabbi was busy talking to Mr. Petrie. "Ever think about getting back into the business, Alex?"

"I never left it," Mr. Petrie replied. "It left me."

"I know, but of all of us, you were the best. Excuse me—you *are* the best!" The rabbi's voice took on a different tone. "You know, performing magic is not restricted to the vaudeville stage. Sometimes when I deliver a sermon, I mix in a trick or two. It's very effective."

The rabbi, it turned out, remembered every bit of Mr. Petrie's history, including the fact that he had an engineering degree. And now the rabbi had a final trick up his sleeve for his old colleague: he would help him get a job teaching high school science. "It's all that physics training that made you such a good illusionist," the rabbi remarked. He handed Mr. Petrie his card and made him promise to call.

On the subway ride back to the Bronx, Mrs. Petrie fell asleep. While Ozzie read pamphlets on magic he'd picked up at the show, I thumbed a *Daily News* that had been left behind. I looked over at Mr. Petrie, studying his framed certificate. He was smiling. He took out the rabbi's card, read it, and tucked it back into his pocket. And then, very softly, he started to sing to himself: "Blue skies, smilin' at me/Nothin' but blue skies do I see . . . "

Mr. Petrie became a science teacher at a Hebrew parochial school in Queens. In spite of the long commute, the Petrie family remained in the Bronx. Mrs. Petrie bought challah and more in my father's bakery, and I continued to visit Ozzie and see Alexander the Great perform.

Uncle Menashe's Magic Challah
Challahs were baked in my father's bakery on Fridays for the Jewish Sabbath and for Jewish holidays, except Passover, during which time no leavened breads are eaten, and the bakery was closed. The challahs were served as part of the Friday evening dinners at home, and were also part of the Sabbath welcome at the synagogue.

Of course, today, challahs are everywhere, and are served as French Toast in countless Sunday brunches. I am always amused when strips of grilled bacon are placed on top, along with the kiwis and strawberries. Uncle Menashe surely would have rolled his eyes at that!

INGREDIENTS
3 packages dry yeast (total ¼ ounces)
½ cup warm water
½ cup plus 1 tablespoon sugar
3 tablespoons butter or margarine
1 tablespoon kosher salt
4 eggs (3 plus 1 for the topping)
5½ to 6½ cups bread flour
1 tablespoon poppy seeds
Canola oil spray

BAKING EQUIPMENT
Two large cookie sheets

PREPARATION
In a large bowl, proof *(activate)* the yeast and a tablespoon of sugar in the warm water. Cover with a kitchen towel and place on top of the stove. Turn on the oven to the lowest level of heat to warm the air around the bowl.

While the yeast is proofing, melt the butter or margarine in a small saucepan. Remove from heat.

Beat 3 eggs in a small bowl; add the salt and the rest of the sugar. Then add to the butter and mix well.

As soon as the yeast has proofed—you'll know because the surface will be covered with a bubbly skin—add the butter / egg/ salt / sugar mixture, and stir.

Add five cups of flour, one cup at a time. Mix well with a wooden spoon after each addition.

When all the flour is absorbed and you have a nice, soft ball of dough, turn it out onto a large wooden kneading board. Add handfuls of flour as you knead, folding, turning and pushing down on the dough with your hands until you have a soft but firm mound.

Grease a second large bowl with a bit of margarine or a spray of canola oil. Place the dough into the bowl, being careful to see that all of the dough gets a bit of oil on it. Cover with a kitchen towel or, if you are eager to see it rise, with clear polyethylene wrap. Place the bowl back on top of the stove for about an hour or so, until the dough has doubled in size.

Remove the dough from the bowl and place onto the wooden board for some more kneading. Make sure you sprinkle the board with flour so that the dough doesn't stick. Knead vigorously. (You want to remove all the air from the dough and have a nice, smooth, non-sticky surface.) Keep adding handfuls of flour during the kneading process. After about five or ten minutes, the dough is ready to be shaped into two braided challahs.

Divide the dough in half, and then divide each half into three parts. Take one of the sections and roll it between the palms of your hands, creating a small rope of dough. Place this small rope onto your board; using the palms of both hands, extend the size of the rope to about 12 inches in length. Do this for all six pieces of dough.

Set aside three of the pieces and braid the other three ropes. Lay them side by side, pinching the ends together at one end, then braid. Repeat the process with the other three ropes for the second challah.

Place each loaf on a large, non-stick cookie sheet (the largest you can fit into your oven) that has been sprayed with canola oil.

Cover with a towel and place each sheet onto the top of the stove for a second rising. This should take about 25 or 30 minutes, or until the loaves have doubled in size.

Remove the sheets from the top of the stove and brush breads gently with a beaten egg. Sprinkle poppy seeds on top of each loaf.

Place in a pre-heated 400° oven, each pan on a separate rack, one pan directly above the other.

About 25 or 30 minutes later, you should check the oven. You want nicely browned, shiny loaves, dark but not burned on the bottoms. When they look right, remove them from the oven and cool on a wire rack for an hour or two, and then devour.

The Bookie's Mistake

Before there was a state-run, off-track betting system, if you wanted to bet on the horses you actually had to go to a racetrack, or you did what many people who had an inclination to bet did—you used a bookie.

My father's bookie was a man named Izzy. I'm sure he had a second name but I never heard anyone use it. The single name Izzy, however, was most often combined with, "the bookie," as in: "Izzy the bookie is on the telephone" or "Have you seen Izzy the bookie?" Of course, if you were addressing him directly, you would simply call him Izzy.

For as long as I could remember, Izzy was always hanging around our family's bakery. Besides an insatiable desire for prune Danish, he had another reason for this, relating to economics. When my grandfather and father had been putting the finishing touches to the construction of their new bakery store in the Bronx shortly after World War I, the telephone company had approached my father and asked if it could install a pay telephone booth inside the store. Public phones were important to the telephone company at that time because not many working-class families had their own telephone service. They relied on the phones in the neighborhood stores.

My father jumped at the idea of a pay telephone booth in the store. Not only would the bakery receive a percentage of all the money that people spent using the phone, but it would cut the number of telephone calls the salesclerks and the bakers were likely to make during working hours, if there was a "free" office phone. The only problem, as my father later found out, was that he had to walk around with a pocketful of nickels at all times. He was like a cashier at the Automat. My mother complained that he always had holes in his pockets from all the coins.

The bakery never acquired its own business telephone. The public pay phone was its only telephone. It rang, and we answered with the name of the bakery. When Izzy the bookie started coming around, it became Izzy's phone as well, and more or less cemented the relationship between my father and Izzy.

It was all rather routine: Izzy would drive up to the bakery shortly after the breakfast crowd had gone. He would seat himself at the table nearest the two large, brass coffee urns, making it easy for him to keep a steady supply of fresh coffee in his cup. Then he would spread out his copy of the *Morning Telegraph* (which he preferred to the *Daily Racing Form*) and study the charts at the various tracks in the area. Before long, the telephone would start ringing. Most of the time, the calls were for Izzy.

In exchange for the use of the telephone, Izzy the bookie became my father's personal, on-call chauffeur. If my father wanted to go, for example, to a cafeteria outside of Yankee Stadium, which was the unofficial meeting place of The Bronx Bakery Owners Association, he would only have to say: "Got a meeting, let's go," and Izzy the bookie would carefully wrap a half-eaten Danish in a paper napkin and hurry out to his car—an old, black Lincoln. Almost as an afterthought, on his way out, Izzie would smile at one of the salesclerks and remind her that if there were any calls for him, to be sure to get the number and tell whomever was calling that he would get back to him as soon as he could. He never forgot that his was a service business.

At least once a day, Izzy would drive my father to the bank with the cash from the previous day's sales. Izzy also drove my father to his pinochle and poker club in Yorkville, or to visit his brother in Passaic or his accountant who had an office in lower Manhattan. He would even drive my father and my mother to the cemetery if either of them was suddenly taken with a need to visit dead relatives.

During these excursions, my father would sit up front alongside Izzy and light up either a Between the Acts Little Cigar or a large cigar, depending on the likely length of the drive. From that point on, my father would issue a series of angry comments about Izzy's lack of driving skills: Izzy was either going too fast or too slow or going in the wrong direction altogether. Interestingly, my father never learned how to drive.

I never thought Izzy was a particularly attractive person: his head was too thin for the rest of his body, and a long, pointy nose dominated his face. His skin was the color of a month-old newspaper that had somehow fallen behind one of the display cases. He had a constantly disappointed look, as if he had just been told he had been permanently barred from the clubhouse at Aqueduct Race Track. His conversation consisted mainly of grunts and one-syllable words. His typical telephone conversation went like this: "Yeah, ten on number three in the fourth. Gotcha."

For a long time, I had absolutely no interest in Izzy the bookie or horseracing or betting. It was just something my father and the bakers talked about with great passion as they shaped a mound of dough into Kaiser rolls. All I knew was that you could win a great deal of money if you bet on a long shot and it won, and you could lose a great deal of money if you kept betting on long shots.

What distinguished Izzy from others in his trade was that he was an independent bookmaker. He was not part of a larger organization. To be specific, he was not connected in any way with the "mob" or any of the "families" that ran bookmaking establishments and numbers rackets in the backrooms of saloons. Izzy was known to these people, but I guess they figured that he was "small potatoes."

There were even times when Izzy—concerned that he would not be able to handle a particularly large bet—would "lay off" a portion of it with one of those mob-run operations. But those times were rare because most of Izzy the bookie's bettors were in the two, five or ten-dollar range.

Occasionally, when there was a big championship prizefight, Izzy would take bets on these events as well. But horses were his main game, and his livelihood depended on knowing when to "lay off" a bet and when to "ride" with it. Even my father admitted reluctantly that Izzy the bookie knew his ponies.

Usually, I would bring my after-school devil's food cake to the table next to Izzy's. By then, he'd be busy recording all the bets that had been called in that day. We never exchanged more than a "Hi" on my part and a grunt and a weak smile on his.

However, on one particular afternoon, I found Izzy in what appeared to be serious conversation with my father.

"I don't know," my father said. "You better be careful. After all, you don't know this guy from a hole in the wall."

"True, but he did come highly recommended." Izzy muttered like a ventriloquist, barely moving his lips. "Schultz from the Bremen House in Yorkville said he's rich from being rich. Lottsa real estate. Owns half a Suffolk County."

"Rich don't mean a thing," my father said, his voice rising. "What's he gonna do, pay you off with a potato farm?"

Izzy turned away for a moment and caught my eye. "Your father is a real pessimist. If Man O' War was racing against a horse from the milk company, he'd want odds."

I looked at him blankly.

"Leave the kid alone," my father said. "This isn't a game."

"I think it'll be fine," Izzy continued, this time directing his conversation to my father. "Look, he's bet with me a dozen times. I never had anybody bet more than fifty bucks a pop. Now here's this guy, with a good recommendation, dropping a hundred every time out. The one time he won, I'd laid off most of it, on account of I wasn't too sure."

"Just lucky," my father said derisively. "Dumb luck."

"Not dumb luck. I figured his horse—even at eight to one—had a chance to win. He came in third a week before, coming on in the last quarter mile."

"All right, so what are you coming to me for?"

"I'm coming," Izzy groaned, "because this time he's got five hundred down on a horse that hasn't even come in the money." At this point, Izzy began searching though some papers that were stacked near his Danish. "I got the dog's whole record for the past year." He proceeded to read from his notes, something like: "Couple a months ago at Arlington, with Arcaro up, this horse—Doomsday—he comes in next to last. Next time out, same track, same jockey, with the lowest weight, he fades in the final turn and comes in sixth in a field of eight. Then . . . oh, I can go on, but it's the same. Good jockeys, little speed, no heart."

This was, by far, the most I had ever heard Izzy the bookie say at any one time.

"So what are you telling me?" my father asked. "That I should tell you he's a sure thing to lose again?"

"I guess so," Izzy replied.

"Well, I'm not gonna say that because you and I know there isn't any such thing as a sure thing. Believe me, I'm talking from experience."

"I know, I know, Nate," Izzy said impatiently. "But this guy is putting up $500 on a horse that's 30 to one. I'd have to lay off at least $400 of that, which would take a bit of doing, and I can do it if I have to. But it would be awfully nice to keep the whole thing. The race isn't until Saturday, so I don't have to make a decision until the day after tomorrow."

"Do what you want," my father said, standing up abruptly. "But don't come to me crying if that plug suddenly gets a new life and wins. Jeezus, Izzy, that's a $15,000 payoff. Where you gonna come up with that kinda money?"

Izzy didn't look happy. He looked over at me; he seemed about to speak to me. I quickly flipped open my elementary physics textbook.

"Leave me out of this," I said.

Normally, I would never go near the bakery on Saturdays. It was bad enough, I figured, that I was expected to help out on Sundays, so Saturdays were my free days—no school and no work. But I was really curious about the race. Supposing, by some miracle, this 30-to-1-shot plug, as my father referred to him, actually won the race?

Assuming Izzy's decision was not to lay off a good portion of the bet, and assuming that he was unable to pay his customer, what then? Would the guy give Izzy some time to make good? After all, he couldn't sue Izzy for the money since betting away from the race track was illegal. And then there was the awful image I had of Izzy being beaten to a pulp, having his legs placed into a pail of cement and then being dropped into the East River. But I was letting my imagination spook me. Probably, the worst that would happen is that Izzy would lose his old, black Lincoln and whatever other possessions he had, and my father would lose his personal chauffeur.

Before I left our apartment, I looked up the racing charts in that morning's edition of the *Daily Mirror*. Sure enough, in the sixth race at Belmont was Doomsday, the horse in question. The formal listing described him as: "Doomsday, out of Sunset by Black Night." The one-line comment by the newspaper's handicapper was: "Lackadaisical performances offer little hope for sudden success." The odds had jumped to 40 to one.

When I arrived at the bakery, Izzy was nowhere to be found. My mother, who was working behind the counter, was somewhat surprised to see me. "What are you doing here? I thought you were going with your friend Irwin to Chinatown."

"I changed my mind," I said as I sauntered to the rear of the store. I went into the back room, my father's office, but it was empty. I asked one of the salesclerks if she had seen Izzy the bookie.

"What do you want him for?" she asked with a smile. "You gonna start betting?"

"Nah, I just wanted to ask him something."

After a short while, my father came up the stairs from the cellar.

He looked at me for a moment. "Looking for some work?" he asked. "I got plenty for you to do."

"No, thanks," I said. "I was just curious about Izzy the bookie. You know, I wanted to know if he laid off the bet or kept it for himself."

My father seemed surprised. "What do you know about bets and layoffs? Where do you come to such things?" he added.

"Well, the other day, you and Izzy were talking . . . "

"Never mind what we were talking . . . who told you to listen in on somebody else's conversation?"

"Well, I couldn't help overhearing and . . . "

"Next time don't listen," he said. "But if you must know, he's a big fool. I think he's making a big mistake." Then he smiled slyly. "They're broadcasting the race at 4:30. Why don't you come back then? We can hear it on the radio in the office."

At about 4:15 I was back in the bakery, and my father and I went into his office. Izzy the bookie still hadn't made an appearance when we turned on the radio. Within a few minutes, the announcers were giving a rundown of the horses in the sixth race. It took a while because there were twelve horses, and Doomsday would be running from the position farthest from the inside rail. He was also the horse with the longest odds. The favorite, Fat Cat, had won his last three races.

My father and I huddled in front of the radio as the race began. We listened as the announcer listed the positions of the horses after the first quarter of a mile: "In the lead is Fat Cat, followed by Willy Nilly and Breathless and Read-To-Me."

There was no mention of Doomsday.

After the first half mile, Fat Cat and Willy Nilly traded places, but there was still no Doomsday. By the three-quarter pole, Read-To-Me had taken the lead; Breathless had apparently run out of air. Fat Cat was still in contention but, again, there was no mention of our horse.

"Do you know if Izzy laid off the bet?" I asked.

"How the hell should I know?" my father said grimly.

The radio announcer shouted: "Now we're coming into the stretch! Still in the lead, it's Read-To-Me and . . . wait, coming up on the outside is Doomsday, eating up the turf, squeezing inside between horses . . . Read-To-Me is fading . . . it's Doomsday. It's Doomsday by a nose!"

My father and I were shocked. How could it have happened?

"Izzy's cooked," my father said sadly. "He just wouldn't listen to me. He made a very big mistake."

"How do you know he didn't lay off the bet?" I asked anxiously.

"I just know."

Suddenly, the radio announcer was shouting again. "Wait a minute . . . wait a minute! We have a challenge!"

My father and I looked at each other.

"Yes!" the announcer bellowed. "Doomsday is disqualified for bumping in the back stretch. The winner is Read-To-Me, paying $4.20 . . . "

"The lucky bastard," my father said. "He could've really been in trouble. He could've dropped twenty thousand. This way he makes the full five hundred."

I was happy for Izzy the bookie.

Within five minutes, Izzy came storming into the bakery. He ran over to my father. I had never seen him so animated. I guessed, he had heard the results and was greatly relieved. But that wasn't the case.

"Dammit, Nate," he said. "You caused me to make a very big mistake. You had me so nervous, I went against my better judgment."

"What are you talking about?"

"What I'm saying is, I laid off most of the goddam bet. I could've kept the whole five hundred. Now, all I'm gonna make is fifty bucks on the deal. What a mistake!"

"Mistake?" my father screamed. "Mistake? You came this close to losing your shirt. If it wasn't for the disqualification, and if you hadn't laid off most of the bet, you'd be in the toilet. Don't you realize that?"

"My only mistake," Izzy the bookie declared bitterly, "was listening to you."

With that said, he turned and left the bakery. I thought it was the last we'd ever see of Izzy the bookie. But on Monday, after school, I found him at his usual place in the bakery, at one of the rear tables, with the late edition of the *Journal-American* spread out under a plate of cheesecake and a cup of coffee.

In the back room, I greeted my father. "I see Izzy's back," I said.

"He's still grumbling that I caused him to make a big mistake, but he's not really stupid. He knows he did the right thing. And where the hell is he gonna get free office space, fresh coffee—*and* his own telephone?"

The Dancing Gypsies

My Mother said
I never should
play with the gypsies
in the wood.

Don't ask me why, but that simple nursery rhyme always made me nervous. From the very first time I heard it, probably when I was about three years old, it conjured up all sorts of scary images of sweet, little, innocent children, lured into a sun-drenched forest by the jolly music of smiling gypsies who, as darkness descended, suddenly changed into gruesome monsters and kidnapped the little darlings, tied them up and probably ate them.

That was when I was three.

When I was seven, I listened anxiously as one of my aunts, for whom I had the greatest love, introduced its chilling words to her four-month-old son as he enjoyed the warmth and nourishment of her left breast. By then, I was big on numbers, and I calculated that that particular parental warning consisted of thirteen words. I knew already that thirteen was a spooky number and should be avoided whenever possible. So it made me even more nervous.

I don't know when I first became aware of the real gypsies who occasionally came into my father's bakery.

For many years, all of the retail bakery shops in the New York area, including my father's, had their copper mixing bowls repaired by a family of gypsies. (In case you do not know it, besides fortune telling and playing the violin, gypsies are by tradition great tinsmiths.) They would come unannounced in the late evening, pick up the bowls that needed repair and return a few days later at a time when my father was likely to be there to pay them. It was on these return visits that I glimpsed them. *These* gypsies didn't appear dangerous, just slightly mysterious and, from what my father said, unpredictable.

But it was probably not until I was about 12 that I completely revised my thoughts on gypsies. That was when I was taken to see a Nelson Eddy movie in which the hero sang a rhapsodic version of Emmerich Kalman's "Play Gypsy, Dance Gypsy." Maybe gypsies weren't so bad, after all?

In the bakery, my father had a series of copper mixing bowls, ranging in size from twenty-four inches in diameter to as much as three-and-a-half feet. The bowls took a heavy beating in the electric mixing machines and, accordingly, needed constant attention. When they weren't being used they sat on a shelf in the cellar, upside down, looking like the domes of an ancient mosque. Whenever the dents or cracks made the bowls too unwieldy or caused them to leak, the bowls were put aside in a corner behind the breadboxes that were used in the proving process. There they would sit until the gypsies decided it was time to collect them.

These copper bowls were costly items, and my father tried to keep using them for as long as he could. Once the war started, new bowls were almost impossible to come by. If there was a choice between producing shell casings or mixing bowls, the weapons won hands down.

To make matters worse, you still couldn't telephone the gypsies if you needed to have your bowls repaired—the way you would the oven man when a steam valve broke, or the rope guy when you wanted a new one-inch-thick hemp line installed for the dumbwaiter. The gypsies did not have a telephone. They came when they came. Unfortunately, the gypsies hadn't been to my father's bakery since several months before Pearl Harbor, and my father was beginning to worry.

Weeks more went by with no sign of the gypsies. My father became more and more on edge. The number of damaged mixing bowls outnumbered the usable ones, and even these were fast deteriorating. To compound the problem, the Easter/Passover holidays were coming up, and my father would need every bowl he could get his hands on. Simply put, my father was desperate for his gypsies!

"It's ridiculous," he mumbled to no one in particular or maybe me, since I was the only other person in his office at the time. The office was a cozy place in chilly March because it sat directly above the bakery's two coal-burning brick ovens.

"You'd think after thirty or so years in America they'd get one lousy telephone. What's with these guys? When you need them, they're never around." He ripped off his apron and threw it onto the oak card table.

"Maybe Uncle Ruby knows how to get in touch with them?"

"Don't you think I called him?" my father growled. "I called everyone—Pato, Friedhoffer, Liebel, Ritter, Brenner, Zaro, Taub. It was all the same. The gypsies come when they come."

"What about Mr. Bartell?" I asked. He was the guy my father went to when he needed steel racks or pans. "Maybe he can fix the bowls?"

"That klutz? I tried him once on some small bowls. I thought I could save some bucks, but they fell apart in no time at all. And it took him forever." My father threw up his hands.

"Well, how did you get in touch with the gypsies in the past?" I asked, trying to be helpful without angering my father.

"You don't understand," my father said, pulling out his *cardboard* box—no one still had *tin*—of cigars from his breast pocket. "These guys are gypsies. Telephones are like bank accounts to gypsies."

"What's so bad about a bank account?"

"Bank accounts mean taxes, tax collectors," my father said, smiling for the first time that morning. "Gypsies want nothing to do with governments, with taxes, with telephones, addresses. They're like no other people in the world," he said. I thought I glimpsed envy in his eyes. "You don't see them working six and a half days a week, getting up at 4:30 in the morning and working twelve hours a day."

"I used to have this idea that they kidnapped little children," I said, laughing. "You know, like the nursery rhyme." I recited it in the singsong manner that I remembered.

My father didn't even stay to hear the whole verse. He picked up his apron and, muttering to himself, made his way to the ovens in the cellar.

Two days went by. We were that much closer to the holidays, and still no gypsies. That evening I saw my father and Freddie trying to hammer out the dents in several bowls and working with a soldering iron that neither of them had the slightest idea what to do with. I strolled by and started whistling, "Play Gypsy, Dance Gypsy." My father gave me one of those watch-your-step-sonny-boy looks that told me I was treading on dangerous ground.

A few evenings later, I was looking through the plate glass window of the bakery, absentmindedly watching the dwindling number of people on the sidewalk, when suddenly at the curb there appeared a rusting, dirt-encrusted, black pickup truck with a cocoon-like canvas rigged over its rear section, much like a covered wagon in a Western movie. The gypsies—six of them—had arrived!

Almost casually, they paraded into the store, single file, and made their way toward the narrow staircase that led to the cellar. I watched as Omar, the father and leader of the clan, followed by his eldest son, Gimi, and the rest of the group, walked by me without so much as a nod.

Omar was a short, bowlegged man with long arms, which were jammed inside two deep pockets in his trousers. His jet-black handlebar mustache made his face look like something you would see in a comic strip. Gimi was a younger, larger, slimmer and straighter version of his father.

Omar glanced around, noticed me and wheeled back. "Where's Korm?" he asked, referring to my father in his Romany version of the family name. I pointed to the office at the back of the store.

"Good," he said. "Tell him Omar's here. We'll meet him downstairs."

I ran into my father's office, pushed open the door and gave him the good news. "The gypsies are here," I announced. "Omar, Gimi, the whole gang!"

My father looked up from his accounts book. "Thank God," he said.

You have to understand that for my father to invoke God was quite a novelty. But I could see he was genuinely relieved that his prayers, or whatever they were, had been answered, if not by divine intervention, at least by Omar. My father reached into his vest pocket and pulled out a formidable, thick, six-inch-long cigar and lit it with great care; then he reached for his apron and made his way to the stairway and the gypsies below.

I followed him. It wasn't often that I saw my father in a mood of such complete joy. Perhaps *ecstasy* might be a more accurate term.

When we reached the cellar, the gypsies were already behind the breadboxes, examining the damaged mixing bowls. My father and I edged closer but were careful not to interrupt their diagnosis. The gypsies, according to my father, were a temperamental group, and, at this moment, with the holidays only days away, he was not about to give them the slightest reason to do anything but fix the damn bowls as quickly as possible.

Finally, after what seemed like an hour but was more likely ten minutes, Omar came out from behind the breadboxes. He was carrying an abacus. Until then, I had never met anyone who ever actually used one. I had thought they were simply ornamental *tchochkes*.

Omar looked grim. "Too many bowls, Korm," he announced.

I wasn't sure what this cryptic message was leading to, but I knew it wasn't good.

"Whatta you mean, too many bowls?" my father said uneasily. "You don't come for six months; that's not my fault. If you had come two months ago, it wouldn't be too many."

"Don't worry, Korm. I never let you down. You're okay," Omar went on. "But with the war and everything, nobody's throwing away an old bowl. You should see what I have to fix."

"All right," my father said with a sigh. "So what's it gonna cost me?"

With a flourish, Omar slid some of the beads on his abacus up and down several times. Silently, he mouthed some numbers and then started to do some more calculating.

"Stop with the violin music," my father said, his voice rising to just below a scream.

"Korm, Korm, please, I'm trying to do the best I can for you because I like you," Omar said, looking for confirmation from his first son. "Gimi, tell Mr. Korm what I said about him when we were driving here."

Gimi looked blank. He put down the large bowl that he was carrying. "I don't remember," he mumbled.

"That's right," Omar said. "You don't remember, but I was telling you and Bodo that of all the Bronx bakers, I respect Korm the most." He repeated it for emphasis: "Yes, respect for Korm."

"Okay, Omar," my father responded more calmly. "So what are we talking about?"

Omar slipped his abacus into his pocket. "You got twelve bowls. Three are in very bad shape. You should throw them away but I know you can't, so I'll fix them but I have to charge you double for them. Twenty-five each for nine; fifty for each of the three." Omar wiped his face with a red handkerchief. "You want to know the total?" he asked.

"Three-seventy-five," my father said without skipping a beat. "That's way too much, Omar. You never charged me more than $15 a bowl. Now you're talking $25 each, and $50 when you decide that you may have to work a little bit harder on a few of them."

My agitated father realized that his cigar had gone out. He searched through his trouser pockets for a match and was frantically re-lighting it when Omar dropped his next bomb.

"Also, I finish in two weeks," he said. I noticed he blinked two or three times as he said that.

"Two weeks?" Are you nuts?" my father screamed. "You guys are all alike. You know you got me over a barrel, so you go for the kill." He took two quick puffs from his cigar. "Put those bowls back. Nobody's gonna fleece me," he said firmly.

When he blew a perfectly round smoke ring, I realized my father's anger was a ploy. He was negotiating.

"Korm, like I say, big respect, the biggest respect," Omar said. "For you, I have a deal." He paused and looked around to Gimi and the others. "I do this only for Mr. Korm."

My father and I waited while Omar milked his dramatic moment. "You know, holidays are coming. Easter for the Christians; the Jews, Passover; Romany—we have holiday, too. Celebrate life. Big midnight feast. We roast whole lamb. We go upstate to Grandpa Tibor's farm. But Tibor is almost dead. He had big stroke. My mother says there will be no celebration there while Tibor is dying." He paused and looked at my father with those sharp, black beams that were his eyes. "You see where I am going, Korm?"

My father looked at me, and I could see he was as bewildered as I was.

"Korm. My most respected baker," Omar went on, this time with great passion. "I make good deal for you. When do you close for the Passover holiday?" he asked.

"The evening of the first night," my father responded. "On Thursday, the second of April. But what's that—"

"Good," Omar interrupted. "We come the next night. Korm, I am going to fix all your bowls by this Saturday for only two hundred. That's very cheap. Good deal for you. For that we roast our lamb in one of your ovens. Is that a good deal?" Omar smiled so broadly that I could even see some of his teeth gleaming under his oversized mustache.

I was shocked at the gypsy's proposal. Surely, my father wasn't going to let him roast a whole lamb in our bread ovens? Wasn't there some kind of health code or something that made that illegal?

But, in spite of my concern, my father did not seem in the least perturbed. In fact, he now blew three more perfect smoke rings, then smiled. "You got a deal, Omar," he said. "But make it a hundred fifty. You can roast your lamb, and you can do a goat, too, for all I care. But you gotta fix all the bowls by Friday. Okay?"

"Okay, Mr. Korm." Omar beamed. He turned to his family. "See, now you know why I have big respect for Korm."

I was still not sold on the whole idea, and I guess something in my face said as much. "Whatsa matter, little Korm?" Omar said, wrapping one of his big calloused hands around my chin. "You not happy to roast lamb? Maybe you like a big fat pig?" He roared with laughter, as did his son Gimi and the other gypsies.

Omar reached for a couple of the damaged bowls and started up the stairs. The others followed, each carrying two bowls.

Later that night, when I knew that my mother could not hear us, I asked my father about the arrangement he had made with the gypsies.

"The oven's going to smell of lamb for a week," I said. "And if it gets out that the bakery was roasting lambs in a bread oven, well . . . I don't think Rabbi Horowitz is going to like a non-kosher lamb . . . well . . . "

"Well nothing!" my father declared. "I'll run the oven with some fresh coal for a couple hours and it'll be fine. You'll see, it'll be fine. But one thing," he cautioned. "Don't say a word of this to your mother."

"Why?" I asked. "She always loves roast lamb."

"Roast lamb she loves, but she hates gypsies," he said.

"Really? I thought . . . "

"Trust me. Not a word."

It was the first time he had ever asked me to lie to my mother, but I figured it was only a lie if she asked me. And the odds were at least a thousand to one that she was not likely to ask me if my father was planning to roast a whole lamb in our bread oven for a bunch of gypsies.

Four days later, on Friday afternoon, well in advance of the Easter and Passover holidays, the gypsies came by in their rusting old pickup with twelve gleaming copper mixing bowls.

When Ruby and the other bakers heard that my father's mixing bowls had been repaired in time for the holidays, they were, of course, delighted, but they had no idea what price he had to pay for this miracle. My father had told no one except Freddie. He knew he would need Freddie to help in "airing" out the ovens after the roasting session. Freddie loved the whole idea and was hoping that they would take up my father's offer to roast a goat, too. Roast goat was Freddie's favorite food.

So, on the third night of Passover, my father and I slipped out of our apartment on the pretext that we were going to go to a high school basketball game up in the Fordham University gym. Freddie's son, my father informed my mother, was on the Fordham Prep team that was playing Mt. St. Michael's, and my father thought it would be nice if we went. My mother bought the story, and I was shocked at how easily she could be lied to.

Of course, we headed straight for the bakery (still officially closed for the holiday). Freddie, who was *not* attending his son's fictitious basketball game, had come several hours earlier to stoke the ovens with fresh coals, which by now would be sizzling shards of crimson and yellow.

Just as my father unlocked the front door of the dark shop, Omar's pickup turned the corner of Vyse Avenue and pulled up. It was followed by a similar truck. There were more than six gypsies this time around. I could see that this lamb-roasting operation was a pretty big deal.

Omar greeted my father and me, while the rest of his group

unloaded a large rectangular iron pan, about four or five feet long, which contained the unlucky dead animal. They carried it gingerly into the bakery and placed it onto the wooden dumbwaiter, which usually carried the fresh breads and rolls from the cellar up to the store.

Only the head of the lamb distinguished it from what could have been a very large skinned dog. It was cut down the middle and spread out in the pan, the feet at the corners. I was not thrilled at the sight. Every spare inch of the pan was filled with onions, turnips, stalks of celery and several other objects that I could not identify. The lamb's flesh glistened from the olive oil that had been brushed into every crevice. The odor of crushed garlic and sweet red wine filled the bakery.

A few minutes later, the pan containing the lamb was resting on a worktable by the fired-up oven. Freddie and my father and two of the gypsies lifted it onto the largest peel that the bakery had, and placed the peel's flat head on the lip of the oven door. They paused for a moment or two while my father and Freddie discussed how they would get the pan into the center of the oven. It was going to be a tricky maneuver but they managed to do it. My father grinned in satisfaction.

That was it! In a few hours, the gypsies would have their roast lamb.

Gimi and some of the other gypsies went back upstairs and returned moments later with a large basket of dried fruit, several bottles of unlabeled red wine, some soda for me, and a large corrugated box, which contained a violin, a concertina, tambourines and the biggest mandolin I had ever seen. It seemed we were going to have a celebration.

And so, while the lamb roasted, Gimi and his relatives toasted my father and Freddie. They passed around the fruit, which they said came from Grandpa Tibor's place upstate, poured the wine (and the soda) and played the most delicious music I had ever heard. One of the group, a cousin of Gimi's, stood up and, between the empty worktables and the equally empty steel racks, danced a dazzling series of twists and jumps that caused even my father to gasp in wonderment.

My father, who could never resist a compulsion to dance at the slightest sound of music, decided to join in and succeeded in winning their respect if not a real appreciation of his dancing skills.

Thus, for the next two or three hours, we ate and drank and danced and sang, and laughed until we were all exhausted—and our lamb was properly roasted.

There was a bit of a struggle getting the roasting pan out of the oven, but once that was accomplished, everyone seemed pleased with the results. After the gypsies loaded the roasted lamb onto one pickup truck and they all drove off to enjoy their midnight feast, Freddie, my father and I cleaned up as best we could. Freddie promised my father that he would come in the next day to air out the oven and clean up one more time, so that even my mother would not have any idea what had gone on in the bakery while Fordham Prep allegedly played Mt. St. Michael in the Fordham University gym.

We didn't arrive home until a little past midnight. My mother was already in bed but she, like all mothers, was a light sleeper. She called out to my father and me as we came into the apartment. "That must have been quite a basketball game. I thought you forgot how to get home," she yelled, showing just the right amount of sarcasm to unnerve us.

"Oh, it was great. Double overtime," I said. "And Freddie's son scored the winning basket."

My father rolled his eyes at my new skill of lying.

"And then Pop took everyone out to Krum's for ice cream sodas."

"That must have been quite a trick," my mother yelled back. "Krum's is closed for the Passover holidays."

I looked toward my father, who was already disappearing into the kitchen.

War Casualties

Getting our copper pots mended was not the only problem my father's bakery experienced during the war. Of course, our home-front inconveniences were minor compared to the life and death struggles overseas.

Still, by 1943, the war had begun to take its toll on the operations of the bakery. The production of cakes containing large amounts of sugar and cocoa was severely limited. The frosting on my devil's food cake, among others, simply disappeared, followed by the cake itself.

The survivors were fruitcakes and pies, coffee rings and babkas. It was not all that bad. Flour, the principal ingredient in the production of breads and rolls, was still being produced in huge quantities in America's heartland, without any restrictions on its use. The Kaiser roll was still king, and no one even thought about changing its name to a "victory roll" or some such nonsense. But I wondered if I would ever taste an éclair or a napoleon again.

At one point, in the spring of 1943, there was an unforeseen shortage of onions. Suddenly, that flavorful bulb was virtually unavailable except if one was willing to pay enormous sums for it on the black market. You could buy two Florida grapefruits for the price of a single onion. So, for a short time, onion rolls became a casualty of the war.

On the other hand, during that fall, potatoes were so plentiful that Mayor LaGuardia, in his weekly radio address, urged housewives to buy up bags of potatoes and store them in their cellars. Few Bronx apartment dwellers could take advantage of this bonanza, even when the A&P took out full-page advertisements in the newspapers offering 50-pound bags of potatoes, packed in special burlap sacks, for the unheard of price of $1.49.

When Hans, one of my father's bread bakers, heard about that, he told my father he had a wonderful Hungarian potato-rye recipe that used equal portions of potatoes and rye and white flours. It sounded like a grand idea, but none of the bakers was thrilled about the prospect of peeling 200 pounds of potatoes.

Mayor LaGuardia also involved himself in trying to ease the shortage of coffee beans. He advised housewives to save their brewed coffee grounds and use them a second time. When Mrs. LaGuardia heard about her husband's proposal, she told the reporters that she had advised the mayor to please stay out of the kitchen.

Every day, the small bakeries around the city were being challenged to come up with new ways to get around the scarcity of butter, eggs, sugar and cocoa. I would hear my father talking with his brother Ruby—who of course, faced the same problems in his Brooklyn business—about how much honey or molasses he could use safely instead of sugar without compromising a piecrust or a sponge cake. Powdered milk and powdered eggs, which had been frowned on for years, were now making headway among the bakers.

While all of these production challenges were being struggled with, there was a moral challenge offered by the black marketeers, who promised endless supplies of sugar, butter and other rationed items. I once heard my father refusing such an arrangement. The following week, the unscrupulous fellow he'd been talking with was the subject of an OPA (Office of Price Administration) sting operation, and he wound up paying an enormous fine.

For my father, the biggest challenge was the butter cookie. He insisted that butter meant butter, not vegetable shortening or—heaven forbid—oleomargarine! So by the time the summer of 1943 had ended, the bakery's production of butter cookies had ended as well.

This situation presented a real problem: since America had entered the war, butter cookies had become the most popular items that families in the neighborhood mailed to their sons in the service. True, most of these cookies must have arrived in more pieces than intended, and they might have had the texture of sandpaper, but they probably were still tasty—and nothing said "home," when home was the Tremont section of the Bronx, more than a star-shaped cookie with a half of a maraschino cherry in the center!

One afternoon, my mother was working in her usual post behind the cake counter when a longtime customer asked her: "So, where are the butter cookies? My David loves them, and I promised him I'd send him some more. You know he's in North Africa, and they don't know from cookies there."

"We just don't have enough butter," my mother explained. "And my husband won't make them with shortening or oleomargarine."

"Do you think my David will know the difference? To him a cookie is a cookie—it's like a kiss from his mama."

That was all *my* mama had to hear. As soon as it was possible to leave the counter, she took one of her rare trips down into the cellar and confronted my father and Gustaf Eagle, the cake baker.

"What's so terrible about using oleomargarine in the cookies when you can't get enough butter?" she asked.

"It's terrible, that's what," my father growled.

"Well, I can't tell the difference," she replied. "And I'll bet you can't either."

"He can," Gustaf declared. "Last month I did a couple a dozen Danish pastries with oleomargarine, and he took one bite and went through the roof."

My father smiled. Either Gustaf was telling the truth or he was trying to flatter my father in a most obvious way.

"I don't care if he can tell the difference," my mother said, talking directly to Gustaf. "What really matters is whether *your* son in Tarawa or Guam—or whatever that place is called—will get to taste a cookie that his own father baked."

My mother knew how to make a point!

So from that time on, whenever the supply of butter ran out or was dangerously low, Gustaf simply substituted oleomargarine in its place. My father, who was an early proponent of "Truth in Advertising," changed the bulletin board on the wall behind the cake counter from "Butter Cookies" to "Fancy Cookies." He figured "fancy" was a better term than "oleomargarine." He'd always had a way with words.

Of course, besides these material changes, the war had a huge impact on every facet of life in and around the bakery. Before the attack on Pearl Harbor, many Americans had been urging the government to do more to save the European Jews. Now, as the young men in the neighborhood were volunteering or being called up to serve in the Army and the Navy, their families were feeling pain as well as satisfaction that something was at last being done, not only to save the Jews but to defeat Hitler and his cohorts.

It seemed, by the fall of 1943, there was not a single family that did not have someone in the service. My cousin Jerry, who was three years older than I, had been drafted into the Army in the fall of 1942. In the few months between his graduation from high school and his call-up, he had been working in a Civilian Conservation Corps program doing "something with machinery." Because of this, the Army sent him to Nevada where he became an airplane mechanic, working on the troop and transport planes that were sent to the Far East. My mother and aunts were relieved that he was not in any real danger, but I was somewhat disappointed that his letters had little in the way of adventure in them, and mainly described the dinners he was invited to by the small Jewish community in Reno.

Now that I was in high school I came to my father's bakery not to do my homework but to work in it. Sundays, I was there all day. The mornings were spent helping out at the worktables in the cellar, and the rest of the day I was upstairs working as a salesclerk. My Uncle Phil, who was the regular night-counterman, never worked on Fridays. So I was drafted (no irony intended) to be the Friday night man. It wasn't all that onerous. Because of "blackouts," it was no longer possible to remain open until eleven o'clock or midnight, which were the old closing times. By nine o'clock, I was gone.

Wartime Fridays along with Tuesdays loomed large for me because those were the days that the *New York Times* reported the names of servicemen who had been killed or wounded, or who were missing in action or prisoners of war.

There was something ghoulish in the way we read and re-read those columns, which listed the dead, the wounded and the missing in action, and their next of kin.

The columns seemed to go on forever. The relatives listed included fathers, mothers, sisters, brothers and wives. Occasionally, the "next of kin" was simply written as "friend." I always wondered if the friend would search through the killed or wounded soldier's papers and call some distant relatives in California to tell them the news.

There was a separate listing issued by the Navy Department, which always had more "missing in action" names than the Army's. Every now and then there would be an update: "FIELD, EDGAR S., seaman, father, Frank G. Field, 170 Thompson St, New York, previously listed as missing in action, is now confirmed dead." I tried to imagine how many days or weeks had passed while the family of Seaman Field wondered whether he was alive or dead. Now that he was "confirmed dead," I thought that perhaps it would have been better if there had never been that hope that he was alive and merely missing.

Often there would be penciled markings made by my father or my mother or one of my aunts next to a name of a soldier from our neighborhood. Occasionally, we would recognize the name of a customer's son. That was always the saddest time.

One October morning, while the Russians were forcing the

Germans to retreat along the Dneiper River in the Ukraine, and the 5th and 8th Armies were pounding the airport near Rome, Freddie received a telephone call from his wife telling him that their son, who was serving in the North Africa/Italy area, had been reported missing in action after his plane was shot down near the Italian capital.

My mother, who had been laying out cookies on a tray at one of the tables at the rear of the store, had answered the call. A voice with whom she was not familiar simply asked for Mr. Martinez. She called downstairs for Freddie, who entered the phone booth in a casual manner. After a few moments, my mother noticed that Freddie was sitting quite still; he was no longer holding the earpiece. He was simply staring ahead blankly.

When she went over to the booth and pushed open the folding door, Freddie slumped sideways into her arms. And then he told her: "My boy's dead." He sobbed out the rest: "They say he is 'missing in action' but I know he's dead."

"You know nothing," my mother insisted. "Missing in action means missing in action. It doesn't mean he's dead."

Freddie's bad news instantly spread through the bakery. I came upstairs in time to hear my mother explain, "Look, he was a gunner on one of those big planes. They take a long time to go down when they're hit. Probably everybody parachuted out."

"Do you . . . do you really think he's okay?" Freddie stammered.

"Of course he is!" my mother said. "The Italians really hate the Nazis and love the Americans. He's probably having a big dinner with a nice Italian family right now."

"God, Lilly, I hope you're right!" He hugged and kissed her, the tears rolling down his face.

All of the bakers were now upstairs to commiserate with their friend. The salesclerks had stopped waiting on customers, and tears filled their eyes. Mrs. Russo, who had been slicing a marble loaf for a customer, pulled out her rosary, which normally was kept warm by her two ample breasts, and began praying.

My father pushed through the crowd that had surrounded

Freddie. "Look, buddy, lemme get you home. You should be with Marie," he said. He looked around. "Where the hell is Izzy the bookie? Just when I need him, he does a disappearing act."

"I'm right here, Nate." Izzy had not disappeared after all. "You want we should drive Freddie home?"

"Of course. Where else should we go?"

"If I drive him home, I won't have enough gas to take you to the track tomorrow. My 'A' ration card is used up."

"So we'll take the subway tomorrow," my father said. "At Parsons Boulevard they have a bus that goes right to the track."

"I don't know where he lives but I don't ride subways," Izzy the bookie continued, trying every which way to avoid using up his "A" ration card.

"Just shut up and bring the car around to the front of the store," my father ordered. "He lives somewhere on Bainbridge Avenue. And anyway, he ain't dead. He can talk." For the first time since he had received the terrible news, Freddie smiled. My father's vaudeville routine with his bookie/chauffeur was always good for a laugh or two.

The next day, Freddie surprised everyone by coming to work.

"What the hell are you doing here?" my father asked. "You should be home with Marie."

"Marie's doing fine; her sister is staying with her. I told her what Lilly said about them all parachuting out, and how the Italians hate the Nazis and love the Americans."

"What does Lilly . . . " my father started to respond, and then he caught himself. If my mother's explanation had been able to convince Freddie and Marie that their son was likely, at that very moment, being feted by an entire Italian village, why should he be the one to deny them this hope? "She's right, you know," he said, trying to sound authoritative. "But I still think you oughta go home."

"Absolutely not." Freddie sounded determined.

My mother's wishful analysis of Freddie's son's situation offered only temporary comfort. As the days went by, I could see that hope was giving way to grief. Freddie was beginning to move around the worktables as if he were being filmed in slow motion.

Several weeks went by; the Allies were moving ahead on all fronts. The American forces in the Gilbert Islands finally took over the Japanese base in Tarawa. (I wondered if Gustaf Eagle's son was enjoying the margarine-laced cookies that his father had baked for him.) The Russians were doing extremely well and were getting deeper into Eastern Europe. The 5th and 8th Armies were marching on Rome, Florence and Genoa. But still there was no word of any change of status regarding Freddie's son.

My mother, who had an epigram for every occasion, called on the old chestnut: "No news is good news."

As we were preparing for the Thanksgiving holiday, even my mother was beginning to doubt that the bakery's favorite gunner was alive. And then, two nights before Thanksgiving, the phone in our apartment rang. It was almost midnight. I was in the kitchen cramming for a mid-term exam in "Meteorology," one of the "war courses" we had to take. I jumped up and ran to the phone. I was sure it was something terrible because no one ever called a baker's family after nine o'clock just to chat.

"He's alive! He's alive!" It was Freddie, and I could feel his joy right through the wires.

"Oh, that's wonderful!" I yelled. My mother, who had raced in from her bedroom, grabbed the phone. She could move like a short-stop when speed was called for.

"Didn't I tell you he was okay?" she shouted. "Oh, Freddie, I am so happy for you."

When we heard the details, I realized that story was very much as my mother had visualized. The plane—a giant Flying Fortress—had been hit during a bombing raid over the Rome Airport, but instead of abandoning the plane, the pilot managed to make a crash landing on one of the very runways that the Americans had been attacking. The airmen had been captured by Italian soldiers, who had hustled them to the Italian compound. Whether the Italians were treating the Americans like conquering heroes and serving them banquets was another matter. Freddie's son was a POW, but at least it was with the Italian army, not the Germans.

My father was very happy. He pulled out a bottle of his favorite J&B Scotch and poured himself an inch and a half. He offered some to my mother and, surprisingly, to me as well, but we both declined. It was well after two o'clock by the time we went to sleep.

The next day I did poorly on the meteorology exam, but who cared? As soon as school was out, I rushed to the bakery to see Freddie.

When I arrived, the first thing I saw was a huge sign in the window announcing that Freddie Martinez's son was alive and well and ending with: "THANK GOD!" The next thing I saw was Freddie. He was smiling for the first time in weeks.

Two months later, Freddie and Marie's boy was freed from the Italian POW camp and was flown home. He had broken several ribs and suffered some internal injuries from the crash-landing, but otherwise he was fine. He sat out the rest of the war at a desk job on Governor's Island at the mouth of the Hudson River.

After the Allied forces opened a second front in Normandy in the spring of 1944, there were many more names of soldiers and sailors listed in the *Times*. The fact that my father and his fellow bakers were running out of ideas as to how to make cakes and pies that resembled their prewar counterparts didn't seem to matter to them anymore.

And then, after weeks of "Maybe they will and then again, maybe they won't," on May 7, 1945 the Germans surrendered unconditionally. The Japanese followed less than four months later. Before we knew it, the supply of sugar and real, honest-to-goodness butter and cocoa and fresh eggs began filling up the shelves near the worktables in the cellar of my father's bakery. Just in time, too, because every Sunday, for the rest of that year and well into 1946, the window of the bakery was filled with over-sized chocolate, butter-cream and whipped cream cakes with wonderful messages: Welcome Home Eddie . . . Welcome Home Louis . . . Welcome Home Daddy

. . . Welcome Home Richard and Robert . . . Welcome Home Christopher . . . Welcome Home Sheldon . . . God Bless Our David . . . Welcome Home Morty . . . Welcome Home Our Hero . . .

The war was over in Europe, in the Pacific and in the Bronx.

Home-front Butter Cookies
(with real butter)

After the war, the butter cookie remained one of the most popular items in my father's bakery. It was the gift you brought someone when you paid a visit, much the way a bottle of wine is used today. The fact is, in the best of all possible worlds, the visitor should bring along both, because they do go well together.

Like most butter cookie recipes, this one is relatively simple. But you will need a piping bag and metal tip if you want to achieve the star-like shape of the bakery cookies that wartime mothers and wives sent to their men serving far from home.

If you insist on cheating, you can adjust the recipe so you can use a cookie cutter according to the direction in the note following this recipe. But you never heard me say that, did you?

This recipe yields 50 to 60 cookies.

INGREDIENTS

2 sticks softened butter (8 ounces)
¾ cup confectioner's sugar
2 eggs
¼ teaspoon salt
1¼ teaspoon vanilla extract
2¼ cups all-purpose flour
4 tablespoons milk
Toppings: maraschino cherries (cut in half) or sour cherries soaked in kirsch, or the jam of your choice. Melted chocolate is a nice topping, too.

BAKING EQUIPMENT
Cookie sheets or baking pans
Medium-size piping bag
#826 piping tip (or similar star-shaped tip)
Parchment paper

PREPARATION
Blend all the ingredients except the flour and the milk.

Add the flour and, using your fingers, blend everything together.

Add the milk and, with a hand-held mixer, blend everything until the mixture is smooth, soft and pliable.

Preheat oven to 350°.

Cover the bottom of baking pans or cookie sheets with parchment paper.

Insert piping tip into the bag; fill the bag two-thirds-full. Hold the bag straight up, with the tip pointed down, barely touching the parchment paper, and squeeze out star-shaped cookies. Cookies should be about 1¼ to 1½ inches in diameter.

Dampen your pinkie with cold water and make an indentation in the center of each cookie. Fill these centers with the cherries or jam. If using jam, make a cone-shaped tube out of the parchment paper, fill with as much jam as you think you will require, cut a snip off the bottom, and squeeze gently. If you plan on chocolate as a center, add a dollop of melted chocolate *after* the baking.

Bake for about 20 to 25 minutes (or longer) until the bottoms of your cookies are a golden brown.

Note:
If you're planning on cookie cutters, reduce the milk in the recipe to 2 tablespoons to make a firmer dough. Form into a ball and wrap in wax paper. Refrigerate dough for approximately one hour, then roll out on a floured board to ¼-inch thickness before stamping out your cookies with the cutters.

This Funny Thing
Called Love

What is this thing called love?

This funny thing called love.

Just who can solve its mystery?

Why should it make a fool of me?

—COLE PORTER

Shortly after my sister, Edith, graduated from college in 1943, she began a career as a copywriter for Gimbel's Department Store, working for the legendary retailer, Bernice Fitzgibbons, the woman who created the slogan, "Nobody But Nobody . . . " The line stood by itself, never needing to be finished because the implication was clear that neither Macy's nor any other competitor could undersell Gimbel's when it came to cotton shirtwaist dresses or floor lamps or boxer shorts or radios or whatever.

My sister's job proved to be a tough one: the hours were long, the deadlines were always "yesterday" and the general pressure to succeed kept her in a constant state of anxiety. It was also wartime.

Most of the men were in the Army or the Navy, and there were no Saturday night dates to relieve the strain of the work or the long, dreary rides on the subway between East 177th Street in the Bronx and West 34th Street in Manhattan. Not even the $21.50 weekly paycheck, the twenty percent discount on personal clothing and the ten percent off everything else in the store could fill that void.

The one bright spot for my sister was Nonie, a young woman from St. Louis who, with her drawing table, T-square, jar of rubber cement, and a wonderfully vibrant personality, shared a tiny cubicle with her. Together, they would create, within a matter of hours, full-page advertisements that would miraculously wind up in all the newspapers that very evening or the next day.

At home, we listened politely to my sister's stories about advertising rates, veloxes (whatever they were), line screens, deadlines, letterpress plates, body text, blue lines, and why "Fitz" liked Bodoni Bold over Times Roman. It was all very bewildering. And mixed in with all of this advertising and typographical jargon, there were stories about Nonie.

For certain, my sister never before had met anyone like her. Nonie was several years older than Edith and was what my mother would describe as "experienced." Nonie was married, and her husband, who had been a sportswriter for the *St. Louis Post-Dispatch*, was a sergeant in the Army, stationed in England. I think my mother had an underlying fear that Nonie would somehow lead my sister astray. My father and I were simply too fascinated by Nonie to care.

Nonie slept with an undershirt that her husband had worn on his last night home before he sailed for England. According to my sister, the smell of his sweat on the undershirt reminded Nonie of their last night together. Frankly, I doubted that she was smelling his sweat—more likely it was mildew. But what the hell, it was kind of romantic, if sweat could ever be romantic.

One day, Edith told us a story about Nonie having cooked a huge pot of sauerkraut with caraway seeds, which was one of her husband

Bill's favorite dishes. She had left it on the stove, uncovered, so that her tiny studio apartment would be permeated with its odors. I said I wanted to meet this woman.

That Friday evening, my sister came home with Nonie. She proved to be everything I had imagined she would be. For one thing, Nonie was gorgeous. She was tall, about five foot ten, with broad shoulders (which I learned later she developed from her participation in high school swim meets), a narrow waist and long arms and legs, which she moved with the grace of a ballerina. She wore her light-brown hair in a thick, single braid that added to her no-nonsense, athletic look. It was clear that she did not take advantage of Gimbel's beauty supplies department, because her luminous skin and pale lips were without makeup. And when she looked at you, there was no doubt that her blue-violet eyes were concentrating on you and you alone. Yes, Nonie was okay.

We were all taken with Nonie; even my mother was won over by her boundless charm. I wondered if Nonie was making a special effort to enchant my mother, as if she knew in advance that my mother had some concerns about the influence she might be having on her only daughter. My mother's total surrender came in spite of two brief incidents. One was when Nonie used the word *fuck* in a passing remark about air-raid shelters—something to the effect of: "Oh, fuck that . . . "

The second time was when my father poured himself two fingers of J&B, and Nonie blithely handed him her glass, with one of those how-about-me-buster looks. She drank hers neat in two or three healthy gulps, which both stunned and pleased my father. From then on, if Nonie was visiting, he always brought a box of cookies from the bakery for her to take home with her.

For the last year and a half of the war, Nonie was a regular Friday night visitor. Some Fridays she stayed over, sleeping on the open-up couch in my sister's room. On those nights, I would hear them giggling well into the early morning. Occasionally, when Nonie walked past my room on her way to the bathroom, I would get more of a glimpse of her than she had intended for me to see. Nonie had small, neat breasts.

During Nonie's visits, we heard a great deal about Bill. And we saw a ton of photographs: Bill as a pole-vaulter at the University of Missouri. Bill with his sister. Bill and Nonie at a Cardinals baseball game. Bill and Nonie kissing, open-mouthed, and with great passion, it seemed. We read clippings of stories that Bill had written for the *Post-Dispatch*. Nonie even read to us the love letters he had sent from overseas. It seemed obvious that the strong feelings of love that Nonie had for her Bill were mutual.

When I was a senior in high school, I got a job as a copy boy for the International News Service (I.N.S.), which was the Hearst Corporation's version of the Associated Press. Now Bill's career and mine were on the same track, even though mine was just beginning. I guess I must have done a great deal of talking about the reporters and editors I was meeting, because one Saturday morning, after a Friday night dinner, Nonie started on one of her stories about what we could all do when the war was over. She and Bill, she said, had this dream about having their own newspaper.

"We figured we could start with a weekly, and then as it grew, we'd be able to raise some money and make it into a daily," Nonie explained with great enthusiasm, spreading her arms in an arc over her head and looking like one of those flowers that—with the help of speeded-up film projection—seem to be blooming before your eyes.

"We could never do it in New York or even St. Louis," she continued. "Too expensive. Bill and I always talked about moving to the frontier—the way people did a hundred years ago. And you know where the frontier is? It's Alaska! What do you think of that?"

Edith, Nonie went on, would be in charge of advertising sales. After all, selling advertising is close enough to advertising copywriting. And Edith's husband—whomever he would turn out to be—would undoubtedly have a literary bent, or maybe he could be the business side, if he was inclined toward business. My role would be to write a column, "Behind the Headlines," or something like that, and I would be the scintillating reporter, creating brilliant pieces of journalism like my heroes of that time—Edgar Snow or Vincent Sheean or Homar Bigart. Of course.

And that's how it went.

Then, one Friday evening, my sister came home without Nonie. Nothing unusual she said, Nonie just wasn't feeling well. So we had dinner without her, and listened to the radio for the latest war news. But I knew my sister, and I could tell that something was up. And it was.

As Nonie had explained it to my sister, she had had a one-night fling with one of the buyers, a married man. She was working late, he was working late, and they were shooting the breeze, and then they went out for a drink, and one drink quickly became two, and two became three, and before she knew it, they went to a hotel, a flea bag on 44th Street, and . . .

"And?" I asked, barely containing myself—angry at Nonie's infidelity to Bill but eager to learn the details.

"And what?" my sister said with a frown. "Do I have to spell it out?"

I gasped. "She's pregnant!"

"No, she's not pregnant. But she feels like shit." My sister rarely used this kind of language so I knew Nonie was in a bad way. Edith confirmed this: "She feels terrible . . . she feels that she betrayed Bill, and she really, truly loves him. And on top of that, she's got this idea that now he is going to be killed in the war, and it will be God's way of punishing her."

"That's stupid," I said. "If God wanted to punish her, He'd kill *her*, not Bill."

"You tell her that," my sister snarled sarcastically. "That'll really make her feel great."

The affair, or whatever you want to call it, passed, and life went on. As far as I knew, that was Nonie's one and only indiscretion during the years that she and Bill were separated.

At I.N.S., I was hearing more and more about the wild goings-on between some of the U.S. troops still in England and British women. Was Bill still in England? I figured that if I was hearing such stories about our soldiers, Nonie was also—and, perhaps, that too was adding to her anxiety.

The war in Europe ended and some of the servicemen came home. But not Bill. He was in Intelligence, and he was needed for the occupation. So Nonie, who, after all this time, could barely get a whiff of sweat out of Bill's undershirt, was left holding it close to her cheek for a few months more.

On the other hand, my sister got lucky. One of the first men to return was my soon-to-be brother-in-law. They met in October, 1945, fell madly in love and were married in January. Nonie was the matron of honor.

Housing was very tight; for about six months, my sister and her husband, Nat, lived with us. We moved the pullout couch from my sister's room into the living room so that Nonie would be able to have a place to stay when she decided to sleep over on a Friday night.

Finally, things started happening fast. Edith and Nat found a place of their own in Queens. Nonie had to get out of her studio because the landlord's son was being discharged from the Navy. The solution to that was easy. Nonie would move in with us, taking my sister's old room. However, before she would do so, she insisted on paying us rent, which my father refused to take but which he finally did take when Nonie said she would not come unless she could pay her way.

And then, the best news of all: Bill was coming home! He was due to arrive on a West Side pier on a Friday, twelve days away.

Nonie was ecstatic. She bought a slew of new dresses at twenty percent off, and even bought a makeup kit. She had her hair styled so that it was no longer in a single braid. She looked radiant. She counted the days. We all did.

The timing of Bill's arrival was perfect, as far as my family was concerned; there would be no problem leaving him and Nonie alone most of the weekend. Friday through Sunday, my father would be at work from five in the morning until eight at night; my mother would put in her three straight ten-hour days; and between school and working all day Sunday in the bakery, I would barely be home. In effect, we were turning our apartment over to Nonie and Bill for most of their reunion weekend.

Nonie took off from work on Thursday and cooked a giant pork roast, sauerkraut with caraway seeds and dumplings. The refrigerator was stocked with Michelob beer, and my father made sure that there was a full bottle of J&B on the kitchen counter. And when he heard that Bill loved lemon meringue pie, he brought two of them home with him that night. Nothing was spared.

Nonie met Bill at the dock when he disembarked that Friday morning. She told us that she did not stop crying in the taxicab until they reached our apartment, and that the makeup she had put on was a total waste because it was all smudged from her tears. But she was unbelievably happy. And so, it seemed, was Bill.

My mother and I were at home to greet them, and we both felt instantly as if we had known Bill all of our lives. The photographs, the letters, the newspaper clippings and Nonie's endless stories had filled in a lifetime.

We left them alone as quickly as we could without being obvious about it. I went off somewhere, I don't remember exactly where, and my mother went to the bakery to work.

During the rest of the three days, my parents and I moved swiftly and quietly in and out of our apartment.

Nonie had hung a do-not-disturb-style sign on her doorknob, the way they do in hotels. She had cut the letters out of newspapers and magazines. It read: "Do Not Disturb—Lovers at Work." It was quite beautiful. I wished I had saved it.

My sister's old room remained, for the most part, dark. Occasionally, we could see a light underneath the door, and we would hear noises, bits of conversation. I was certain that one night, around two in the morning, I heard Nonie singing softly—or was it moaning? All of us tiptoed around the apartment.

When my father and I bumped into one another Saturday evening in the kitchen, he rolled his eyes and nodded toward their bedroom. "Do you think they'll ever come up for air?" he joked.

I noticed that the happy couple had eaten very little of the pork or the sauerkraut or the dumplings. The pies remained untouched. Only the Scotch needed to be replenished. My father opened a fresh bottle of Chivas Regal, which was his celebration drink. He poured himself one before going quietly into his bedroom.

At seven o'clock Monday morning, my mother and I were having breakfast (my father had gone to work as usual about five) when the door to my sister's bedroom opened and Bill came out. He was dressed in his uniform but he hadn't shaved, and he was carrying his army duffel bag.

We stood up when he came into the kitchen, as if we knew he had something important to say. He wasted little time. He talked directly to my mother. "I'm leaving now, and I just wanted to thank you and your family for the hospitality you have shown me these past few days." He started to leave, but turned and spoke again, this time looking at no one in particular. "And I really appreciate the care you have taken of Nonie."

Before he could depart, my mother walked toward him. "Where are you going? Isn't Nonie going with you?"

"I'm going back to St. Louis. Where I'll go once I get there, I really don't know. I have some family, cousins, in San Francisco. Maybe I'll settle there. As for Nonie and me, that's been over for a long time, even before the Army. I guess she thought—no, we *both* thought—we could get back to where we were ten years ago. I did love her then, you know."

"But all those lovely letters you wrote? She read them to us, and they were always about how much you missed her and loved her," my mother said in a quiet, questioning tone.

"Maybe I was just hoping . . . you know . . . hoping things would be the way they once were," Bill stammered. Suddenly he looked old. He was no longer the pole-vaulter, the dashing sports reporter, the handsome lover. "I don't know what to think," he said. "I have this idea about going to law school on the G.I. Bill. I wanted to talk to her about that . . . but she's still fantasizing about starting a newspaper, moving to Alaska, the frontier. Like any of that makes any sense."

I felt a little embarrassed when he said that. I had kind of liked the idea.

"Well, you do what you have to do," my mother replied, resigned to the situation. And then she uttered one of her patented phrases: "Remember, one door closes, another opens." It was her way of ending the conversation, which I knew was painful to her.

A moment later, Bill was gone.

My mother and I sat there trying to prolong the breakfast, wondering what to do. She stirred her cup of coffee, repeating: "I never would have believed it. I never . . . "

Finally, Nonie came out of the bedroom. She was dressed in her regular working clothes, her hair was back in a single braid, and she was wearing no make-up. She greeted us with a cheerful, "Morning," and strode over to the kitchen sink. She pulled Bill's T-shirt—the one with the smell of his sweat—out of the pocket of her jacket and held it over the sink with one hand; with the other she reached for a box of wooden matches, lit one and torched the shirt.

"Funny the way things turn out," she said with a shrug of those broad swimmer's shoulders.

Nonie stayed with us for about five or six weeks more, and then one day she announced that she had taken a job with a fashion agency in Chicago. We had a tearful farewell. At my last meeting with her, she gave me a drawing she had once done of me, and signed: "With Love, from someone who knows all about it."

"I'm going to miss you, Nonie," I said.

"Me, too," she replied. "But promise me one thing. Don't ever be discouraged about falling in love with someone. It's really what it's all about, you know."

My sister kept in touch with Nonie for a few years. They wrote to one another, and occasionally they spoke on the telephone. And then it became Christmas cards.

John's Secret

My father found John the way other people stumble across a stray cat in the backyard, bring it a saucer of milk and suddenly find that they have a new member of the family. John came into our family carrying a pail of coal.

Exactly how that happened is a bit complicated. When my grandfather and father had been seeking a Bronx site for their bakery, a major attraction of the building they eventually chose was its two massive brick ovens in the cellar. They were fueled by coal.

The weekly coal delivery was a messy affair that started with a coal truck that had an iron chute hooked to its back. Coal was poured down the chute through the bakery's cellar doors into a wooden coal bin below. No matter how skillful the deliverymen were, a good deal of coal would often land on the sidewalk. Usually, one of the truckers would grab a shovel and sweep the loose coal into a large pail. A porter from the bakery would then carry it downstairs by hand.

Only on this particular occasion, in the spring of 1921, there was no porter around, so the pail of coal sat on the sidewalk.

My father, who had come out of the bakery to check on the delivery, was reluctant to soil his clean white apron. For a moment he thought about walking away from the coal (it was no more than a few dozen pieces). Then he spotted a forlorn-looking young man observing the scene. Figuring he had nothing to lose, my father yelled across to him, "Hey you, you wanna work? Take this pail of coal down to the cellar." My father must have used some hand gestures to reinforce his words because, as he soon found out, the young man spoke almost no English.

The guy nodded, grabbed the handle of the pail and followed my father into the bakery and down the cellar steps. That first task accomplished, my father found several other jobs that needed doing. One thing led to another, and John—that was his name—became a regular fixture around the bakery.

At first, he did only menial jobs: sweeping, cleaning, loading heavy sacks of flour onto shelves, spreading sawdust on the tile floors on rainy days—that kind of stuff. Actually, most of John's time the first few weeks he worked at the bakery was spent scraping the crumbs off pans.

In the 1920s, there were no Social Security benefits or payroll taxes to be withheld. So John simply did what he was asked to do and was paid in cash once a week. Nobody seemed concerned if he was being paid enough, but since he never complained and was always ready for more work, my father assumed he was doing the right thing.

Communicating with John was a problem. He rarely spoke, and when he did, it was only to say, "Okay" or "No." That went on for a couple of weeks, during which time my father attempted to talk to John, using his few words of German, Polish, Hungarian and Yiddish. Eventually, he did determine that John was Russian. "Russky? Russky?" my father had asked. "Da, Russky," John replied. And that was that, at least for a while.

My grandfather and father had long been used to dealing with their non-English-speaking bakers, among whom were three Hungarians, two Poles, one Swede, several Germans and twin brothers from Rumania. No Russians. But, in spite of the language barrier, they were able to determine that John had been a cook on a

Russian merchant ship that happened to be in the port of Baltimore at the very moment that Lenin had arrived at the Finland Station in St. Petersburg. Rather than return to Russia, a number of the sailors, including our John, jumped ship. Exactly how he made his way from Baltimore to the Bronx was lost in translation.

However, the fact that John had been a cook was good news for my father. Like most of the German-style bakeries of that time, my father's store offered a few cooked items for a morning snack or lunch. The menu was simple, consisting of scrambled or fried eggs, American or Swiss cheese sandwiches and, of course, slices of any of the cakes or pies.

My father had lost his regular cook in the move to the Bronx, and he hadn't as yet found anyone to replace him. So John was pulled from his main work as pan scraper to the much more prestigious job in the small kitchen.

Several years went by; the Depression was at its worst, the coffee-and-cake crowd had dwindled, ranging from a few for breakfast to almost none for lunch. But my father and grandfather always found things for John to do. Soon he was busy coring strawberries for strawberry shortcakes, chopping onions for onion rolls, slicing peaches and apricots for pies, polishing the two giant coffee urns that my father would not part with, no matter how bad the coffee-and-cake business had become, and cultivating a small vegetable garden in the alleyway behind the store. John also wheeled a push-cart of baked goods to a commission bakery on Tremont Avenue, which resulted in a conflict with the Teamsters Union. But that's a story you've already heard.

Perhaps all these jobs were not enough for John; maybe he missed being a full-time cook. Because by the time I became aware of him, when I was about six or seven and began to spend my after-school hours in the bakery, he had become a daily, falling-down drunk.

But he was family.

The drinking had not overtaken him all at once. It was more of a gradual thing. At first, I eventually gathered, hardly anyone had noticed. And even though his occasional absences from work were, as my father put it delicately, "a pain in the neck," neither he nor my grandfather gave any thought to actually firing John. I guess they figured they could never really fire him since he had never really been hired. They were inclined to ignore the odor of stale beer that he carried with him as he swept the floor of the back room. My grandfather smiled benignly whenever anyone complained about John. If he was annoyed when the sergeant from the local police precinct called and asked him to please remove John from the reference section of the storefront public library up the street, he never said so. But my mother and my aunts complained often.

When my grandfather died in 1939, my mother saw her chance to get rid of John, once and for all. But by then, my father had become John's most loyal defender. "Please, Lilly, where's he gonna go?" my father pleaded. "If he can't come to the bakery, he might as well be dead."

"So? So what's the difference? As far as I can see, he's been as good as dead for years. A lot of good he does around here." My mother could show no mercy as long as she believed the facts were on her side.

"Have a little pity," my father would mumble and stroll down the cellar steps to check on his precious ovens.

John stayed.

When I was very young, I was spared the coarser, more obnoxious aspects of John's life. No one let me tag along on any of the expeditions where I might have viewed John dead drunk. To me, he was a gentle fellow who patted my head rather than pinched my cheek the way some of the bakers did. And he fussed over me when I was doing my homework. Charlotte Russes or custard éclairs would appear alongside my textbook; later on, when I was in high school, my advanced algebra workbook or a novel by F. Scott Fitzgerald would lie next to a neatly sliced inch of devil's food cake, silently placed there by John.

I managed to converse with him the way my father did, using a kind of pidgin English with a great deal of body motion. But I never did find out anything more than my father had about his early life, whether he had ever been married or had any children. What was it like to be on a merchant ship that far from home? And where exactly had that home been?

One other puzzling thing about John was his habit of collecting scraps of metal. He kept an old orange crate near the worktable where he chopped his onions. Into this crate he tossed whatever worn-out tools or pots and pans or used motor parts that he found lying about in or near the bakery. Wire coat hangers, fragments from old radios, bicycle and automobile parts, handles from metal doors, bed springs, broken-down toasters, alarm clocks that no longer rang, a rusted meat grinder, a much-dented flugelhorn that had lost its valves, and an assortment of twisted flatware—all found their way into John's orange crate. During the war, everyone in the bakery helped John fill his crates, figuring that their contents would eventually make their way to the war effort. Whenever a crate was filled, he would drag it out of the store, presumably to a junkyard where he would exchange it for money. At least that's what I thought.

As the war dragged on, John's heavy drinking bouts actually became less frequent; he managed to get drunk only about once a week. When this happened, he would simply pass out, usually in a warm spot near the ovens. Occasionally, when John appeared to be unsteady on his feet, my father would ask me to walk him home. I guess he was afraid that John might collapse in front of a trolley car, and that his bloody death would somehow become his fault.

These stumbling walks home weren't too bad; John always entertained me along the way with what I assumed to be Russian folk songs. Maybe they were love songs because occasionally John would be crying by the time we arrived at his home. John lived a few blocks from the bakery in the basement of a small factory building that also contained Lombardi's luggage repair business on its ground floor. It was probably illegal for John to be living there but nobody really cared, least of all the Lombardi brothers, who owned the building.

Some time in the early '30s, the brothers had cornered the market on luggage and pocketbook repairs for the major department stores in the city. I remember my mother's cousin Rose telling her how much better the luggage repair service at Bloomingdale's was than at Macy's. Of course, I knew that they both used Lombardi's—only Bloomingdale's probably charged Cousin Rose more than Macy's would have done.

Anyway, once we arrived in front of Lombardi's factory building, John quickly sobered up, thanked me for walking him home and hurried into his basement apartment. I wondered, more than once, as I walked back to the bakery, if John was the recipient of Lombardi's old and battered pocketbook frames and luggage handles.

Pretty soon, the war was over and business was booming. But there was a potential problem. My father's bakery remained one of the few retail shops in the neighborhood without air-conditioning. "If we don't do something soon," my father surmised, "we might as well close up shop." So, for two weeks in August 1946, the bakery went on a sort of "vacation" to allow a contractor to install new showcases, a new window display case and air-conditioning in the upstairs sales area.

When the bakery reopened with a huge red and yellow sign in the window that read: FULLY AIR-CONDITIONED, we felt as if V-E Day had arrived all over again. Everyone except John. He had been on a solid two-week binge while the bakery was being refurbished. When he came back to the bakery and felt the first chill of the new air-conditioning, he consumed a fifth of vodka in less than an hour and staggered out to his vegetable garden in the alleyway behind the store, where he fell asleep in the sweltering heat.

The next morning, Freddie found him lying unconscious near the ripening eggplants. Freddie called for an ambulance and then called my father. My father and the ambulance from Fordham Hospital arrived at the same time. Once John was in the hospital, the doctors determined that he had pneumonia along with an assortment of other problems, mainly having to do with his much-abused liver.

Over the next two weeks, almost everyone from the bakery took turns visiting John, including my mother, who brought him a small cactus plant. In her own practical way of thinking, she would rather bring someone a plant than flowers because "plants have a longer life." When I visited him later that same evening, John told me that my mother's visit had meant more to him than any of the others because he was aware that she had never approved of him. He pointed to the cactus and smiled. "Beautiful, no?"

It would not have mattered if my mother had brought him tulips: two days later, John's liver gave out. Someone from the hospital called my father at the bakery to say that John had died and that my father had been listed by John as his "next of kin."

As my father was attempting to make the funeral arrangements, we realized how little any of us really knew about John. We assumed that he was Russian Orthodox, and we called the Russian Orthodox Cathedral of the Ascension on Bathgate Avenue, the only Eastern Orthodox church in the Bronx. Nobody there had ever heard of John, but they said they would take care of the burial.

There was no ceremony. Everyone who truly cared about him had made it to the hospital.

A week or so later, my father received a call from the captain of the 48th Precinct. The Lombardi brothers wanted John's stuff moved out of the basement apartment. The captain said he would meet us there. My father and I walked to the Lombardi building and waited a few minutes for the captain to arrive. My father recognized him as one of the regulars from the stationhouse who came by for a free birthday cake a couple of times a year.

"Nasty business," the captain commented, getting out of the dark green Ford that was the official police car in those days. "I got the key here," he muttered as he pulled it from his inside pocket. "I don't think this should take too long."

"I don't know how long it will take," my father said. "I never been inside." He turned to me. "Have you ever?"

"Nope," I answered. "I never got beyond the front door. You know, come to think of it, John wouldn't even open the door until I was on my way. It was like he never wanted me to see what was inside."

"Now I'm really curious," my father said, laughing. "Maybe he's got a distillery in there."

When we entered the place, it was almost completely dark; the window shades had been drawn. For a few moments we could not find a light switch. When we did, the sight was so shocking that no one said a word for at least ten or fifteen seconds. What we discovered was that John had done very little for the war effort. He had not sold the old scrap metal he had collected to make bombs. In fact, it was all here.

The low-çeilinged room, which must have measured about 30 feet by 30, was crowded with the most fantastic creations we had ever seen. (The only ordinary things were a tiny cot and a table loaded with tools.) The objects were at once grotesque and whimsical. John had transformed all of the broken gears, the battered pots and hubcaps, the crushed sheet metal and the glistening tubes of plumbing pipes into a series of dazzling sculptures.

"Jesuzz, will you get a load a this crap," the captain said mockingly. "It's worse than a junkyard."

Neither my father nor I was ready to respond. Instead, we walked purposefully through rows of objects that were stacked on long, raw-wood tables. Some of the pieces were as much as three or four feet high and stood by themselves on the floor; others were the size of a coffee pot. We recognized in the welded forms old trays that had once held displays of butter cookies, a part of a metal lampshade that had been a fixture on the round oak table where my father did his bookkeeping, and one of the arms from a ceiling fan near the ovens that my father had replaced several years before. We even found the ancient coal pail, the one that had brought John into the bakery on the day he had started work over a quarter of a century before. John had turned it upside down and had attached to it twisted bits of wire hangers so they looked like flowers blooming in a pot.

As we moved slowly from piece to piece, I discovered what must have been John's last creation. On top of a cone-shaped bedspring, he had attached a large letter B. It looked like the star on top of a Christmas tree. The letter had been part of the word BAKERY, which had just been demolished in the remodeling of the window cases. John had obviously taken it from the dumpster placed outside the bakery a few weeks earlier.

Finally, my father spoke, directing his words to the captain. "I don't know what to say. It's all so crazy. I figured there'd be some old clothing and few sticks of furniture." He rubbed his hand against the small wheel of a child's tricycle. "Tell Lombardi he's gotta give me a week, and then I'll clear out this stuff. It's not like I can load it up into a taxi and take it to the Salvation Army."

"Yeah, I know what you mean," the captain said. "You go ahead, and I'll talk to Lombardi. When you need the key, just give me a call."

On our way home, I told my father that I thought there was something to John's crazy sculptures. "I don't know if it's art, but a lot of things that pass for art these days look like junk."

"So what do you think we should do?" my father asked. "You have any bright ideas?"

"Well, we have a week to think of something."

For the next two days my father was unusually quiet, almost introspective, if that was possible. One morning, I saw him having a serious conversation with our landlord over coffee. When they finished, my father was smiling and Mr. Schulman, who usually had a scowl, appeared to be quite pleased with himself.

My father beamed. "It's settled," he declared. "I've arranged with Schulman to let us bring all of John's sculptures here and set them up in the garden behind the store. It was really John's garden, you know. There was nothing there until he started putting in tomato plants."

I realized that my father had made a very personal appraisal of John's work. He had referred to it as "sculptures," not junk or scrap metal. I still didn't know if you could call it "art," but that was another matter.

"That's not all." My father chuckled. "I got that cheapskate to drive his truck up to Lombardi's so we can pick up all the pieces."

"That's great," I said. "But how'd you get Schulman to do that?"

"He and his wife are celebrating their thirty-fifth wedding anniversary in a couple a weeks, and they're having a party. I told him I wouldn't charge him for the cake," my father said. "He figured it's a good deal."

The next day, Mr. Schulman, his partner, Dave Altchek, my father and I drove to Lombardi's factory in an empty produce truck and waited for the captain to bring us the key. While we sat, I noticed that the small basement windows were covered with newspapers. I thought it was odd but I really didn't know what to make of it.

A few minutes later, the captain arrived and walked with us to the door of John's apartment. "Sorry to be late," he said, smiling. "But I guess there's no rush. This stuff ain't going anywhere, that's for sure."

The captain was wrong. The Lombardi brothers must have gotten their dates mixed up or, more likely, they really didn't care. John's apartment was totally empty. Not a nail, not a piece of a metal coat hanger was to be seen.

My father and I were stunned. Even the captain seemed shocked. "That sonavabitch Lombardi," he said. "I guess he sold it all for scrap metal."

"This is terrible," I said. "Maybe we can get the stuff back? After all, the place was supposed to be ours for a week."

"I'm not too sure about that," the captain said. "I know I asked Lombardi for a week, but he really was under no obligation . . . "

"Well, that takes care of that," my father said sadly.

I was too angry to say anything.

Schulman and Altchek, jumped back into the truck.

"We'll walk," my father said.

I don't think we said a word to one another until we got back to the bakery. "Any ideas about what to do with John's vegetable garden?" he finally asked.

Freddie attempted to keep John's garden going for a week or so. But he didn't have much interest in it, nor did anyone else; within a month, all the plants had withered.

The Genius

My mother's cousin, Rose Greene (the lady who preferred Bloomingdale's repair service to Macy's), lived with her family in Riverdale in a big stone house that overlooked the Hudson River. Riverdale is actually in the northwestern corner of the Bronx, and it remains a beautiful, relatively green enclave. My father used to say that Riverdale was right below Yonkers, a statement that happens to be true, but which he made in order to annoy our Riverdale relatives, who regarded Yonkers as being even more déclassé than the Bronx. They wanted nothing to do with Yonkers—*or* the Bronx. The return address on their letters always read, "Riverdale, New York."

Since there was virtually no public transportation that would enable us to get to Riverdale from the east Bronx, the usual routine was for the Greene family to drive down to see us. The group included two of Rose's brothers, as well as Rose and her husband and their two children. It was always a party when they came. My mother, who was particularly fond of Rose—whose snobbery never got in the way of her good humor—would cook all of her specialties, and the Greene family would return home with shopping bags full of breads and cakes from my father's bakery.

For me, these visits were an opportunity to try to better understand my cousin Jamie, who was only four months older than I but who, by the time I was 12, was three years ahead of me in school and played the piano like a young Paderewski. I never did make sense of him, but I didn't dislike him. I regarded him as some sort of exotic creature.

Jamie was always "up to something." Early on, I became aware that he lied a great deal. I concluded that he enjoyed lying. It was usually about unimportant things. On one visit, Jamie and I went off by ourselves to the Bronx Zoo. When we returned home, Jamie told his mother we had gone to the library. His mother smiled, and Jamie embellished his lie by inventing a story about the librarian who told him that he could not borrow a book from the adult section because he was too young, and how he had pulled out his I.D. card from the Bronx High School of Science, which showed that, even though he was only12, he was qualified to use the adult section. That made his mother smile even more.

Later in the day, after they had gone home, my mother asked me about our visit to the library. "I thought they were closing it for the summer and were going to fix it up," she said.

"It *is* closed. That was just Jamie making up a story."

"Telling lies, you mean," my mother said. "How could you just stand there and let him lie through his teeth?"

"I thought it was funny. And anyway, Cousin Rose seemed really happy that he could use the adult section."

My mother walked away, murmuring something about how glad she was that I wasn't a genius like Jamie.

I never knew whether Jamie was indeed a genius, but as far as his mother was concerned, he was destined for some kind of greatness. My mother would tell the story about the time (midway into her pregnancy with me) she had visited Rose in the hospital the day after Jamie was born; Rose had said, as she held the day-old, five-pound Jameson Charlemagne Greene in her arms: "He will be a physician!" That was greatness at that time in the Bronx. And knowing Rose, my mother never doubted the accuracy of her prediction.

As far as I was concerned, I would have been satisfied if Jamie could catch a baseball or at least sink a foul shot when I dragged him over to the schoolyard to play with some of my friends. But Jamie was totally uninterested in any sports and, try as I might, I knew he would never change, no matter what my friends said.

"Cheez, he throws like a girl!"

"How can he hit the ball if he closes his eyes when he swings?"

"Did you tell him he has to dribble the ball if he wants to run up the court?"

I tried to protect him by telling everyone that he really had to be careful not to damage his hands because he was planning on becoming a concert pianist. The boys seemed to understand that and allowed Jamie to watch us play our games without further derision.

As the years went by, Jamie's world grew more distant from mine. It took him only three years to complete four years worth of high school. So, while I was beginning my second year in high school, Jamie, at 15, was already a freshman at Columbia College—not quite the youngest Columbia student ever, but close enough so that there was a story about him in *The Bronx Home News*.

I began to see less and less of Jamie. His advanced standing as a student and his flippant attitude regarding honesty made any real relationship difficult. Once, when the Greene family was visiting, I asked Jamie if he could help me get ready for a chemistry quiz that was coming up. After all, I figured, he was a college student and a future doctor, so he had to know his chemistry. It turned out that Jamie found the sample quiz questions as puzzling as I did.

"I was never really good in chemistry," he confided. "I cheated on every exam I ever took."

"You cheated?" I was stunned. Here's this so-called genius telling me that he cheated on all his chemistry exams.

"Sure. I cheated every chance I got." Jamie's grin was a tight grimace that pulled the skin across his teeth. "I knew I had to get an 'A' in all my science classes if I was to get into med school, so I cheated. It was easy. At Bronx Science we were on the honor system, so half of us—the ones who were planning to go to med school—we all cheated like crazy."

Could that be true? I couldn't be certain, since the only thing I knew for sure was that I was talking to a consistent liar.

From that point on, I would make some lame excuse that would get me out of our house on the Saturday afternoons when the Greene family was due to visit. If this annoyed my mother, she never showed it. Even she was beginning to find Jamie's precocity somewhat difficult to endure. And it wasn't all that easy for her to listen to Cousin Rose's litany of Jamie's academic and artistic achievements. Occasionally, my mother would mention some minor accolade that had been tossed my way, but she did it without much enthusiasm.

Jamie zipped through Columbia in three years by taking 18 credits a semester and a full program during the summers. His only concession to this crushing regimen was that he more or less gave up a serious interest in playing the piano. I thought this was a shame because Jamie was good. He never cheated with a Chopin nocturne or a Brahms sonata.

The closest I ever got to Columbia was when a group of us from my high school newspaper, *The Evander News*, went to a High School Press Association convention that was an annual event of the Columbia School of Journalism. Jamie met me there for lunch and introduced me to his friend, Lionel, who was already a senior at age 19. Both of them were extremely thin—emaciated might be a better description—and each wore tight-fitting black trousers and turtleneck sweaters. Lionel's pale gray face was severely pockmarked from acne, but it was his perpetual sneer that did not make me want to get to know him better. But Jamie seemed completely in awe of Lionel, laughing hysterically at every mildly off-color remark he made—although I didn't think anything he said was particularly funny.

I was delighted when Hannah Holtzman, who was the editor of our high school newspaper, came by and reminded me that I was due at a seminar on newspaper makeup. As she said this, she looked disdainfully at Jamie and Lionel.

"This is my cousin Jamie and his friend, Lionel," I said. "They're students here at Columbia."

Hannah looked unimpressed as I continued: "Jamie's the same age as I am and he's already. . ."

Hannah cut me off. "We gotta go." She took me by the arm and half dragged me away. "What a bunch of creeps!" she said, as soon as we were out of earshot.

"How can you say that? You barely said hello to them."

"Can't you see they're homos?" Hannah said fiercely.

The use of the word "homo" to describe a homosexual was definitely a pejorative. This was not at all like Hannah. I always believed she was a really nice person; she was rarely in the habit of calling somebody a name.

"Oh, I don't know about that," I said. "Jamie's always been a bit of a sissy, but that's all. He was never into sports . . . but I don't know if he's . . . a . . . you know . . ." I finished lamely.

Hannah was unconvinced.

"All right," I said. "I'll admit Lionel looks a bit weird. But as a journalist, you can't go around categorizing people without some kind of proof." I was quite proud of my defense of Jamie, especially since I was up against the most intelligent girl in Evander Childs High School.

Hannah shrugged her shoulders. "Believe me, I'm right."

"Proof . . . where's your proof?"

"All right, I'll give you proof." Hannah stopped walking and looked straight at me. "Do you think I'm pretty?" she asked.

"Well, well sure," I admitted. Girls were not in a habit of asking me if I thought they were pretty. As a matter of fact, I thought Hannah Holtzman was not only beautiful but smart. I truly lusted after her, but I knew it was hopeless: she was two years older than I and she had a ton of guys who took her to concerts at Lewisohn Stadium or Orchard Beach. I had even heard she had a boyfriend in the Navy.

Hannah accepted my evaluation of her as if she expected it. "You see, even you think I'm pretty. Guys look at me all the time, and I can tell that they're interested in me. But I'm afraid your cousin, Jamie, and his goofy-looking friend looked straight through me. They found each other much more interesting."

I didn't know how to respond; Hannah did it for me. "You see, you know I'm right."

At that moment I wasn't about to argue any further with Hannah. She smiled smugly as we entered a large lecture hall where the seminar on newspaper design was about to begin.

When Jamie finished at Columbia, World War II was just ending, and the colleges and universities were flooded with returning GIs. There was some question as to whether Jamie, who was all of 18, would be accepted into medical school. But his grades were exceptionally good, particularly in chemistry. He was accepted at several medical schools, including the University of Chicago, which was the one he chose.

At first, Jamie wrote me tearful letters about how out of place he felt as a teenager, sharing classrooms with students who were already in their twenties and thirties. Many of them were married, and some had children. There were a few female students, but even if Jamie had been interested in them, he was no competition for the returning veterans. I showed his letters to my mother, who sighed.

It took Jamie the standard three years, but he graduated from medical school and earned a coveted internship at Bellevue Hospital in Manhattan.

There was a big to-do in the stone house in Riverdale when Jamie returned home as a full-fledged M.D. Cousin Rose pulled out all the stops for the huge party she made to celebrate. She suggested to my mother that we could celebrate my graduation from NYU at the same time. My mother graciously rejected Cousin Rose's offer, saying that she was planning her own party for me. That was the first time I had heard about it, but I was happy that I was not going to be a footnote to Jamie's much grander accomplishment.

As it was, I was feeling pretty good about myself. I had finished college, had a real research job at International News Service and had acquired an apartment on Thompson Street in Greenwich Village. I even had a girlfriend, another researcher I had met at work.

Cousin Rose's party was a terrific affair. A huge banner arched across the street in front of the big stone house, painted with the words: "Welcome Home Dr. Greene!" All of the Greene family's neighbors came, and Cousin Rose told anyone who would listen the story of how she had predicted to my mother the day after Jamie was born that he would become a physician.

Cousin Rose also made a big point of introducing me, along with Jamie, to all of the guests. "Oh, Judge Samuels," she gushed to a large man who kept peering at his pocket watch. "I'm delighted you could come." She turned toward me. "This is my Cousin Lilly's son. You know, they have the bakery near the zoo." Then she turned to Jamie. "And this is my son, Doctor Greene."

I thought her formal introduction was pretty funny, but when I told my mother about it, she scowled. "If she thinks I'm going to start calling him Doctor Greene, she can forget about it."

That night, I told my new girlfriend, Gloria, about Jamie. I managed to present a rather one-sided picture. "Here's this guy," I said, "same age as me, fairly well-to-do family, already a doctor, a brilliant pianist . . . " (actually, I hadn't heard him play for at least five years), "and already starting his internship at one of the prime teaching hospitals in the country."

I could see the wheels turning in Gloria's curly, brown-haired head. Her eyes glazed over; clearly, images of her single girlfriends were flitting through her thoughts. Maybe she was even thinking of ditching me for Jamie?

"Perhaps you have a friend who might like to meet him?" I asked, impressing her with my clairvoyance.

"Huh? Oh, yeah," Gloria said.

Gloria narrowed the field to Enid, a woman she knew from college who was working for a music publisher and was studying voice at Juilliard, and her cousin, Frances, who was gorgeous and worked for the Museum of Modern Art in its sculpture department. Culture and beauty all wrapped up into one package.

I realized immediately that, before this went any further, I ought to check with Jamie. For all I knew, Hannah Holtzman's assessment might have been on target. So, the next day, I called and asked him if he would be interested in meeting one of my girlfriend's girlfriends.

"That would be terrific," Jamie said with enthusiasm. "You know, I don't have much time to meet any women except nurses, and they're all so dumb. It would be nice to meet a woman who's interested in something besides bedpans." Jamie could be awfully intolerant of people whom he thought were not his social or professional equals. I wondered what he said about me when I wasn't around.

A week later, Gloria, Enid (the voice student from Juilliard) and I waited for Jamie in the small dining room off the bar of the Old Garden Restaurant on East 29th Street. We figured this was convenient for Jamie, who would be coming straight from Bellevue on 31st Street.

Frankly, I was still worried that Hannah had been right about Jamie, and Gloria would really be angry with me for misleading her and her friend. But within minutes of Jamie's arrival, I was convinced that I had been wrong to even think that Jamie was anything but completely, unequivocally heterosexual.

Jamie was charming, and Gloria's friend, Enid, was—how does Jane Austen say it?—*smitten*. I was really pleased, and I thought Gloria would be, too. Surprisingly, she didn't look all that happy.

After we took Enid home (Jamie had to be back at work in Bellevue's Emergency Room by midnight), Gloria laid it all out for me. She was not one to mince words. "Look," she said, the anger seeming to build up in her throat like the steam in a teapot, "I know you meant well, and Enid is too naive to see through him, but, face it, your cousin Jamie is a fag!"

"Wait a minute," I said. "How can you say that? You just met him, and he didn't say or do anything to indicate that he is not heterosexual."

"Look," she said. (I hated it when she started every sentence with the word, *Look*. I knew it meant that she was about to unload a barrage of bricks.) "Look, a woman, any woman, if she's thinking clearly and is not just hoping for the best, can see these things."

Good grief, I thought, Hannah Holtzman returns!

"You mean, he didn't look at you and immediately send out signals that he lusted after you," I said in a knowing way.

Gloria grinned. "You got it! You saw the way he looked through me."

"Well, I know he didn't pay much attention to you, but I thought it was because he was concentrating on Enid."

"Bullshit. If you really think about it, he talked mostly about himself, mainly about how smart he is, and dewy-eyed little Enid just lapped it up. The more he talked, the more she swooned like the kids who faint when Sinatra sings."

"So he talked about himself. How does that make him a homosexual?"

"That in itself doesn't make him a fag—but you realize he hardly glanced at Enid. And you have to admit she's got a great body."

"I never noticed," I said innocently.

"Don't lie to me. I saw the way you ogled her when she was reaching up for her coat." She smiled. "But that's okay as long as you don't touch."

"I think we ought to let things play out," I said. "Enid may be naïve, but if it's so obvious to you that Jamie is a . . . fag . . . I mean, homosexual, she'll eventually find out." I was desperately trying to smooth things over. I certainly didn't want anything to come between Gloria and me.

As it turned out, it didn't take long before we knew where Jamie stood regarding Enid. Although he had made a big to-do about getting Enid's phone number at our dinner in the Old Garden, a month went by and Jamie never called her.

A few weeks after that, when the Greene family was visiting my folks in the Bronx, I came up from the Village and asked Jamie about Enid.

"Enid? You mean your friend's dumpy little friend? You didn't think I'd waste my time with her."

"But you sure gave us the impression you really liked her."

"Look at it this way. I made her feel good for a couple of hours. It was all an act. You know I'm a pretty good actor."

I was finding Jamie more and more difficult to accept. I also decided that Hannah Holtzman and Gloria were probably right about him.

Jamie finished his internship and began a residency in gastroenterology at Bellevue. As far as I knew, there were no women friends, or any particular male friends in his life. And then, one day Jamie called and suggested he and I have dinner together. Once again, we went to the Old Garden.

Jamie was late, but he seemed genuinely apologetic. Was he putting on an act for me? Our dinner conversation was, more or less, a typical Jamie monologue. He went into boring details about hospital politics, about the pettiness of the administrators, the stupidity of the nurses and his fellow residents, and the total incompetence of the doctors who were supposed to be training the residents to be practicing physicians.

Listening to Jamie, I knew I would never put my trust in anyone in the medical profession.

As the evening wore on, I began to wonder why Jamie had wanted to have dinner with me. As he made his way through three very dry martinis, his conversation became even more one-sided and high-pitched, with a turn toward the loudly vulgar. People at nearby tables began to stare at us disapprovingly. But Jamie went on describing in vivid detail vaginal and rectal examinations, botched tonsillectomies, gory leg amputations, and assorted ruptures of main arteries caused by brutal knifings and gunshots. Where was all this leading?

At last, Jamie told me. He really, truly, hated anything that had to do with blood, intestines, veins and body parts in general. So his mother's dream of him becoming a surgeon had become impossible for him to achieve.

"I didn't know you had to be a surgeon," I said. "I thought being a doctor was enough."

"No, the surgeon part sort of developed along the way. The closer I got to actually becoming a doctor, the more specific she became about what I should specialize in. A surgeon is the ultimate as far as she is concerned."

"So what do you want to do?"

"Psychiatry," he said.

"Sounds good to me. It's a real up-and-coming medical specialization," I said, trying to show some knowledge of the contemporary workplace.

"It's more than that. It's something I really love."

"That's great!"

"Yes, I love the power it gives me over people. After all, these troubled idiots come to me, bare their souls and actually listen to what I have to say." Jamie smiled that taut grimace I remembered from his college days.

"Jamie," I said. "I don't think wanting power over your patients is really a good reason for being a psychiatrist. I would hope that . . . "

"And I love listening to their pathetic little stories. It's like going to a party and hearing the most salacious gossip about your friends. I love gossip. That's why I'll make a great psychiatrist!"

From that point on, I don't think I listened very carefully to what Jamie was saying. His monologue went on through dessert and coffee, and then after-dinner drinks, which I skipped. I was strictly a one or two sweet-vermouth-on-the-rocks drinker then, and I had already passed my limit. But I did manage to hear him say near the end of the meal, as the waiter started to bring us the check, that he had just become engaged.

"You're . . . er . . . you're getting married?" I stammered, unable to stifle my shock.

Jamie laughed "That's what you usually do after you get engaged."

"I . . . I didn't even know you were seeing anyone."

"Well, I guess it is kind of sudden. We've known each other for a few years, but we only started seeing each other seriously a few months ago."

"Well . . . I . . . I thought . . . " I mumbled.

"You thought I was a fag," he said with a huge grin.

"Oh, no, that's not . . . "

"Don't give me that shit. We've known each other too long and too well." He looked around to see if the other diners were still listening to our conversation. But they had already lost interest.

Jamie continued, "I've been a homosexual since I was a kid. I didn't really know what it was all about until I was in Columbia. You remember when you came for that journalism convention? I was with Lionel. God, what a mess he was! But our relationship was wonderful for me, and it gave me my first understanding about who I was."

I listened as Jamie rambled on, describing his struggles with his homosexuality and his acceptance of it finally. I nodded a few times and, when the waiter came by again, I asked for my third sweet vermouth.

"Okay," I said. "I'll admit I'd pretty much figured you were a . . . er . . . homosexual. But if you are comfortable with it, why are you getting married?"

"Good question. One, I want to make a lot of money. Two, I'm not going to succeed as a psychiatrist if I'm labeled a fag. Having an attractive, intelligent wife is necessary for referrals in the circles I want to work in."

"But what about this woman, the one you're engaged to? What happens when she finds out it's all a cover?" I asked, choosing my words very carefully.

"Leslie's no problem. She knows who and what I am, and she loves the idea. The two of us are perfect for one another. She's a travel writer. She's also a lesbian, and she needs a husband as much as I need a wife."

We paid the bill and gathered up our coats; I walked Jamie back to Bellevue. On the way, he asked me how I was doing.

He even asked, "How's what's-her-name—Gloria?"

"Oh, she's doing fine. Moved out to Los Angeles to take a job with a television station, doing news. It's a big break for her."

"Good for her. And how is her friend, Enid? A really nice girl—I should have gone out with her. Maybe we could have made something of it."

"What are you talking about, Jamie? You just got through telling me you are a . . . that you like being one . . . that you're getting married but it's only an arrangement . . . and now . . . "

"But Enid was really a nice person. Very beautiful, great tits, and smart, too," he said. "I probably could have made it with her."

The next day, I called Gloria at her office at KNBC-TV and told her about Jamie. "Three months," she snickered. "I'll give 'em three months, not a day longer."

"Frankly, I was thinking maybe six months."

Then Gloria started laughing hysterically.

"I know you think it's funny, but it's quite sad in a way," I said.

"I agree," Gloria said. She seemed to be trying desperately to stifle her laughter. "I just thought of something," she said. "A poem I once heard. Actually, a limerick. It's perfect for Jamie and his new friend."

Then Gloria recited her limerick: "There was a young fairy named Bloom/Who took a lesbian up to his room/And they argued all night/As to who had the right/To do what and when and to whom."

I had to admit it was funny.

"Isn't it great?" Gloria asked. "I haven't heard it for years, but I remembered the whole thing. I'll send it to you."

A few days later, I received a picture postcard of the Hollywood Bowl; on the other side, Gloria had carefully printed the limerick. I still have it tucked away somewhere.

Jamie and Leslie were married a few months later; they remained a couple for almost a year, so I guess my prediction was more accurate than Gloria's. My mother was surprised when they divorced.

She had long thought that getting married would be the best thing for Jamie. "Maybe he wouldn't be such a sissy," she had said.

I never did tell my mother that the whole arrangement was a lie.

Soon after his divorce, Jamie left the medical profession. He became an antiques dealer. At first, Cousin Rose was very upset, but when he became one of the most successful dealers on Rodeo Drive in Beverly Hills, she was almost as thrilled as if he had become a surgeon. Instead of calling my mother to report on Jamie's near-perfect grades in chemistry, she'd call to talk about a Tiffany table lamp with a flowered glass shade that Jamie had just sold to Bob Hope. Or was it Zsa Zsa Gabor?

My mother took it all in stride, but every so often she would say how glad she was that I wasn't a genius.

Arnie, Or Is It Armando?

Besides the bakers and many of the salesclerks who had become like family to me over the years, there were a number of highly skilled craftsmen who were essential to the smooth running of the bakery.

These included the hard-to-come-by mechanics: the father and son team who repaired the ovens, the gypsy tinsmiths (you remember Omar and Gimi), and Prigal, the Polish carpenter for whom no bread box was beyond salvaging.

I had gotten to know all of them. They had come from eastern and southern Europe, and somehow found their way to our area of the city, bringing with them ancient wisdom that managed to keep modern appliances and machines purring through the Depression and the wars.

One of my favorites was a man I knew simply as Arnie, Arnie the electrician, whose impeccable English was enhanced with a sliver of an indefinable accent that was both exotic and romantic. Once, when I was about ten or eleven, and I was assisting my father in laying out trays of butter cookies, I asked him, apropos of nothing, if he had any idea where Arnie was from.

"He's a Satter," my father mumbled.

I hadn't the faintest idea where Satter was, but I knew enough not to bother my father with too many questions that did not relate to a particular chore at hand. If, for example, we were mixing up a batch of pastry dough, I could interrupt his train of thought as much as necessary: "Two quarts of egg yokes or two-and-a-half?" I could ask questions like that all day long because the wrong amount of egg yokes could throw off the whole recipe. But the location of Satter did not fall into that category of necessary questions. So my curiosity about Arnie would continue unanswered for a while longer.

That evening I asked my mother if she knew where Arnie came from.

"Wherever it was," she purred, "you have to admit he's a well put together man."

Frankly, I wasn't used to hearing my mother talk about a man in this way, but I had already come to expect this kind of behavior when it came to Arnie. My mother, who seemed to be in control of any situation, would suddenly take on the role of a helpless female whenever Arnie came to our bakery. She would giggle at a perfectly innocuous remark from Arnie's finely-molded lips. She once blushed when Arnie told her how nice she looked in a new apron.

Arnie had this way with every woman he met. The mysterious accent, the sparkling eyes, the sensuous smile and, of course, his wardrobe. He was always elegantly groomed. Long before it became the fashion, Arnie dressed entirely in black: a black turtleneck shirt, a black leather vest and narrow black trousers. His dark shining hair reached to his shoulders. My mother's assessment of him was more than accurate.

Needless to say, the women salesclerks, all on the far side of forty, swooned when he came to examine a misbehaving ceiling fan.

All of this meant nothing to my father; my father liked Arnie because he was an excellent electrician whose rates were substantially lower than other electricians'. The reason for that was simple: Arnie did not have an electrician's license. Whatever he knew, he had learned from doing. For insurance purposes, he would get one of his certified electrician friends to swear that he had supervised the work. Actually, licensed electricians often called on Arnie if they had a problem they could not solve. He was that good.

Anyway, my obsession with Arnie's heritage continued. A week or so later I asked Uncle Menashe if he knew where Arnie was from.

"He's from Yorkville," he said as he deftly slid a 20-foot peel into the bread oven to retrieve a batch of rye breads that were in danger of getting scorched. His answer didn't exactly address my basic question, but it would have to do. Uncle Menashe was serious about his baking.

The mystery of Arnie's country of origin remained unanswered for several more years.

Then, one night, as I was busy washing down the display cases and counters in the bakery and preparing to close up for the night, Anna, a salesclerk who had gone home several hours before, returned. Her hair, which had been tied into a neat bun when she was working, was hanging loose, and I could see that the top buttons of her shirtwaist dress were open, displaying a great deal more of her breasts than I was accustomed to seeing.

"I think I left my pocketbook in the drawer," she explained as she slipped past me and reached under the cash register. She opened what was referred to as the "Girls' Drawer."

"Ah, thank God it's here!" she squealed in relief. "How could I have forgotten it?" While she checked the contents of her pocketbook, I turned away and saw that there was a man waiting for her to come out. As I watched him, he looked directly at me. It was Arnie. He gave me a sheepish smile and shrugged his shoulders.

Anna saw that I had recognized Arnie; she became even more flustered than before. "Gotta go now," she said hurriedly. She paused and whispered: "Be a good kid. Don't tell your poppa."

"Don't tell him what?"

"Just don't tell him anything," she said, fleeing out the door.

The following Wednesday, I went to the bakery after school. I made it a point to stop by on Wednesdays because it was the only day that Gustaf, the cake baker, made his devil's food cake, due to the wartime restrictions on cocoa. I placed my geometry book next to the cake plate in front of me, contemplating which I would attack first. But I was distracted by the voices of my father and Arnie, who were in the back office arguing over a bill.

Predictably, my father's arguments began to wear Arnie down; before long, the electrician conceded defeat. He slouched his way out of the back room and sat down with me. Even in his work clothes, he looked as if he was ready for a dance floor. "How you doing, kid?" he asked as he seated himself across from me. Before I could answer, he asked me how Anna was.

"She's okay, I guess." I was surprised that he would be so open about it. "She doesn't work Wednesdays, or you could ask her yourself."

"I know, but I thought she might have said something to you about me," he said in disappointment. "I tell you, kid, she's a very passionate woman."

"Really?" I said, surprised, because I didn't think of older women as having much passion.

"You don't know much about women, do you?" he asked.

"Not really, I guess. I've got plenty of time," I said by way of excuse. "Right now I want to get through geometry. You know, with the war and everything, we're taking more science and math than history and English."

Arnie didn't seem to be listening. "Where I come from, people get married and have kids while they're still in their teens," he said.

I saw this as an opportunity to find out, finally, where Arnie was from. "Where exactly is this place?" I asked as I carefully sliced another inch from Gustaf's marvelous devil's food cake.

"Malta," he said. "You heard of *The Maltese Falcon*—well, that's where I'm from."

"But if you're from Malta, why are you called Satters?"

"Who said anything about Satters? People from Malta are Maltese."

"That makes sense," I said. "But when I asked Pop where you were from, he said you were a Satter."

Arnie smiled broadly, and then he began to laugh. "Jesus, he sure got that one screwed up. Let me tell you something, kid. I don't think your daddy hears so good or he ain't as smart as I think he is."

Arnie leaned forward and returned to a more serious mode. "Your old man was giving me a hard time about me and women. You know, telling me I ought to settle down, stop screwing everything I can get my hands on. So I told him I was a satyr—that's S-A-T-Y-R. Do you know what a satyr is?"

"You mean those guys who are half man and half goat in Greek mythology?"

"Exactly. But it's also a medical term for men who have an insatiable desire for sex with women. The fact is, we can never get enough sex." He looked around to make sure that no one was in earshot of our conversation. "I tried to tell your old man that I couldn't help myself. If I saw a woman, I had to have her."

I must have stopped eating my devil's food cake because my mouth was wide open; I stared across the table at Arnie.

"Close your mouth, kid. I have to tell you, it's not so great. Because as much as I get, it's never enough. I wake up in the morning thinking about sex."

This was getting interesting.

"Fortunately," Arnie went on, running his fingers through his hair, "I'm a pretty good-looking guy. Women seem to go for me, and it's never been a problem finding a woman to go to bed with. Hell, the other day I was up on a ladder, trying to hang a chandelier, and this woman, the one I'm doing the job for, asks if she should stand by in case I slip. I said, Okay, but the next thing I know she's rubbing my ankle. Nice looking lady. Before you know it we're on her couch."

"Wow." I slapped my forehead. "Wow!"

"Stop with the 'wow.' I see you really don't know that this is a sickness. A doctor I went to said it was some kind of psychological disorder. He said I was a satyr, a male nymphomaniac. So, in a sense, I'm some kind of maniac."

"I wouldn't say that," I said, hoping to give Arnie some solace. "But what happens if you don't find a woman who wants to help steady your ladder? Do you go, you know . . ." I hesitated, " . . . do you go to prostitutes?"

"I can always find a woman. I have never needed to pay for sex," Arnie said proudly.

I closed my geometry text. Who could concentrate on right angles and rhomboids when Arnie was confessing to being a male nymphomaniac? Finally I said: "I'm sorry."

"That's okay, kid. But your father must have misunderstood when I tried to explain this to him. He must have been thinking about how many pans of prune Danish he should bake and got things confused. The fact is, I'm a Maltese satyr." He began to laugh. I laughed, too, and then went back to my devil's food cake and my geometry.

I don't think I saw Arnie after that until one Saturday morning in 1951, when I drove my prewar Plymouth from Greenwich Village up to the Bronx to visit my family and the bakery.

I found Arnie sitting at one of the coffee and cake tables, eating scrambled eggs and a buttered roll, reading the *Daily News*. He looked the same as ever, dressed immaculately, every hair in place. He was still, as my mother had said, "a well put together man."

I stood across the table from him for a few moments until he looked up. "Hey, look who's here!" he exclaimed. "Gosh, it must be ten years."

"I don't think it's that long, but long enough. You're still the best-looking electrician in the Bronx. Maybe a few more gray hairs, but you look terrific."

"Yeah, I'm still the same guy, but I'm no longer doing electrical work except for your pop. He's convinced himself—and me—that I'm the only one he trusts." He laughed, dunked a portion of his roll into a steaming cup of coffee. "I'm in the restaurant business. I always loved cooking, and when the chance came to get this place real cheap, I jumped at it. I got the only Maltese restaurant in the city." He paused for a moment to attack his scrambled eggs. "You should come some night. Bring a date. I'm easy to get to, near the stadium on 161st Street. I'm even a better cook than an electrician."

"Sounds good to me," I said. What's your place called?"

"*Armando's.*" He handed me a card with the name and address of the restaurant. "Like I say, come anytime, and the wine's on me."

"Who's Armando?" I asked.

"That's me. I was always Armando, until your pop called me Arnie. You know, I don't think he hears too good. When he recommended me to his brother and some of the other bakers to do their electrical work, he told them my name was Arnie. So Arnie I became. It's worked out pretty good because it keeps my two worlds separated. In the electrical business, I'm Arnie. In the restaurant, I'm Armando."

"I thought you said that you gave up the electrical business except for Pop."

"Well, not entirely," he said, grinning. "There are a few beauty shops and a knitting store that I still service."

"*Service?*" I asked with a sly smile.

Arnie (or was it Armando?) laughed.

A week or so later, I called Arnie and told him I would be coming to his restaurant on Friday at eight o'clock, and that I'd be bringing a date as he had suggested.

"Wonderful!" he bellowed into the phone. He was like many of the "older" generation, who did not entirely trust the telephone's ability to transmit sounds across distances. "You're gonna love it."

On Friday, I picked up Gloria Assael, who had, more or less, become my girlfriend. All the other women at Hearst's I. N. S., where I still worked, were secretaries—except for a couple of the syndicated columnists. Gloria was bright, pretty and somewhat unconventional. Her people were Jews who had been smart enough to flee Italy before Mussolini made it difficult for them to remain there. Everyone thought she was sweet and timid; I knew better. She saw herself as a young Anna Magnani, the sexy Italian actress, and she had a mouth on her that could make a bleacher fan blush. She was fun, and I liked her.

As we made our way up the East River Drive, I told her about Arnie and his unfortunate mental disorder.

"You're kidding. You mean this guy has this insatiable sex drive and he always manages to find women who can give him some pleasure?"

"Yup." I thought uneasily that maybe I had told her too much about Arnie. We hardly said a word to one another for the rest of the trip. At one point, as we approached the turnoff to the Major Deegan Expressway, I gave her a quick side glance; she was deep in thought, smiling ever so faintly, her eyes wide open and staring straight ahead.

The bar area of Armando's was filled with a lively, animated, bordering-on-the-raucous kind of crowd. Many of its occupants were women in their twenties and thirties; it was not a common sight in those years for groups of women to hang out in bars. From their enthusiasm, I guessed some had come during the "Happy Hour" and stayed on.

The table staff, more than half of whom were female, darted deftly in and out of the thirty or so close-together tables, carrying platters of bubbling veal piccata and osso bucco. The food smelled wonderfully rich.

"Shit, this is great," Gloria remarked.

I knew then that she was in raring-to-go form.

After a few moments of surveying the smoky scene, I spotted Arnie; he stood at one of the tables halfway toward the rear of the restaurant, chatting with a foursome as he prepared to open a bottle of red wine. As he talked, his eyes never stopped scanning the room. That's when he spotted Gloria and me. "Hey, don't go away!" he shouted, waving the still-corked bottle. "I'll be there in a minute."

We watched as Arnie finished opening the bottle and poured a few drops of wine into one of the glasses, then waited patiently for the drinker's approval. Getting a satisfied nod, he filled the rest of the glasses at the table—the ladies' glasses first, of course.

I marveled at his expertise, as if he were a born maître d' and had been doing this all of his adult life.

Moments later, I was introducing Arnie to Gloria, who responded to him with the sweet side of her personality. I thought Arnie held her hand a trifle too long as he led us to the one unoccupied table in the rear of the restaurant.

When he left to bring us menus, Gloria turned to me. "He's really quite nice," she said demurely. "For an older guy, of course."

"Of course," I said, showing some sarcasm.

We had a grand time. The food was excellent, basic Mediterranean, with a touch of Middle Eastern—reflecting, I guess, Malta's location just off the coast of Sicily and smack in the middle of the Mediterranean sea lanes.

But the most fun was watching Arnie—or to be more precise, Armando—work the crowd. He joked with the men and charmed the women. The ideal host.

It was also obvious that the restaurant business was not a hindrance for what Arnie needed most in life.

When it was time for dessert, Arnie (I couldn't get used to calling him Armando) sat down at our table and talked about the old days at the bakery, about my father, about me as a kid. But whatever he was saying, his eyes were never off Gloria.

I started to get a funny feeling, but I put it out of my mind.

Arnie was true to his word. The wine was on him, and he added after-dinner drinks as well. When he left our table to handle some crisis in the kitchen, I asked Gloria, "Well, what do you think?"

"I agree with your mother," she said. "He's a well put together man."

A few days later, at work, Gloria told me that she had gotten a call from Armando.

"How did he get your phone number?" I asked. "And what the hell did he want—as if I don't know?"

"Well, for your information, while you were in the men's room, he asked me for my number and I gave it to him."

"Why the hell did you do that? You knew he's a sex maniac!"

"I gave it to him because I felt sorry for him," Gloria said sweetly. "And all he called to tell me was that you are a really terrific guy and I should treat you nice."

"That's it?"

"That's it."

"Maybe he's cured," I said without much conviction.

Lil & Phyll

"They're closing the Y," my wife, Eleanore, said as she entered our apartment on Bronx Park East one evening in March of 1958 and flung her coat over a chair. "I more or less expected it, but not so soon."

My mother groaned. "How awful. All those kids with no place to go after school. It's not a good thing." My mother had been babysitting while Eleanore worked two afternoons and evenings each week as a social worker, running the teen program at the Young Men's and Young Women's Hebrew Association (YMHA & YWHA) on Freeman Street in the southeast Bronx.

"Oh, don't worry about the kids. The Y has made an arrangement with the Boys Clubs of America to take over the facility," Eleanore said.

"It still won't be the same," I said with a sigh. I had come out of the bedroom a few minutes earlier after looking in on our one-year-old daughter, now blissfully asleep after putting her grandmother and me through a vigorous test of wills. We had won the battle but lost the war. Both of us were now thoroughly exhausted.

"No, it won't be the same. The emphasis will be more on athletics than character development," Eleanore mused.

"So why is the Y pulling out?" my mother asked. "Aren't there enough kids?"

"Oh, there are plenty of kids, but they're all the wrong religion," I said. "It used to be all Jewish, now it's predominantly Negro and Puerto Rican. As long as there were even a few Jews, the Federation supported it, but now . . . well, it doesn't make sense."

"Well, I don't blame the Y," my mother said. "Let's face it. If all the money comes from the Jews, at least a few Jews ought to get some benefit from it."

Her tone was matter of fact. Figuring she was on safe ground, she continued talking. "Yeah, the *schwarzers* are all over Freeman Street, the whole Crotona section. It won't be long before they take over Tremont, too."

I could seen Eleanore rolling her eyes as my mother rambled on about the changing nature of the neighborhood.

"Really, Mom, do you have say *schwarzer* ?" I said angrily.

"You very well know that it's just German for 'black.' It was never disrespectful. A Negro man was a *schwarzer*; a Negro woman was *schwarze*," she argued. "We said *schwarzer* in Yorkville. You say Negro. What do you think Negro means?"

My mother had long been a puzzle to us. On the one hand, she could be quite sympathetic about the plight of the Negroes (as African-Americans preferred to be called back in the 1950s). Once, when she returned from a wedding of one of our relatives in Baltimore, my mother told us stories of how badly the Negroes were treated in that Southern city. What especially had disturbed her was the behavior of her beloved uncle, Laurenz, who had tipped the Negro waiter at a restaurant by placing a handful of coins into a dish that previously had held mayonnaise. She had applauded Eleanor Roosevelt when the First Lady had denounced the Daughters of the American Revolution after it barred Marion Anderson from its concert hall in Washington. She had listened gleefully to her first baseball game on the radio when Jackie Robinson became a major league player. And she had also been quite vigorous in support of my father's hiring of a Negro cake baker just after World War II, a first for a retail bakery in the Bronx.

On the other hand, my mother certainly knew that the use of the word *schwarzer* meant a great deal more in the Bronx of 1958 than simply the German word for *black*. I'd been uncomfortable with her using it for years, and Eleanore had pointed out to her the offensive tinge of the German slang, and more than once. But still she persisted in using the terms—maybe just to get a rise out of us.

Disgusted, Eleanore escaped temporarily into the bedroom. When she returned a few minutes later, she picked up the original conversation: "Harry wants to give the teenagers some kind of positive Jewish experience before we leave," she said.

Harry Katz was her boss, an old friend who was the much admired director of the Y. "You know, for the most part, the Negroes see Jews as the shopkeepers who overcharge them, and as their landlords. And everyone hates their landlords!"

My mother sighed. "How true."

"So what does he have in mind?" I asked.

"Well, it's almost Passover, so he thought it would be kind of nice if we had a real Passover seder for the teenagers. He's already spoken to the rabbi from Young Israel on Southern Boulevard, and he's sure he can get the minister from Bethany Baptist to participate. We'll do the whole thing: matzo ball soup, gefilte fish . . . "

My mother interrupted. "I'll make the fish."

"Oh, you don't have to make . . . "

"I'll make the fish!"

"That'll be too much work, and there's no reason for you to do it. They can buy jars of prepared fish," Eleanore said.

"That stuff has no taste. If you want them to have a 'positive Jewish experience'," my mother said, echoing Eleanore's words, "you can't serve them gefilte fish from jars!"

"But there'll be about seventy kids. That's a lot of fish."

"This is important," said my mother. "I don't want these people to see Jews as just thieves and landlords."

Eleanore gave up. But I could see she was worried that my mother would say something like, "It's so nice to see all you *schwarzers* gathered here for this seder," although I knew she never would.

As I drove my mother home that night, she was uncharacteristically quiet. Finally, she broke her silence. "I'll need about 20 pounds of fish. Half and half—pike and white. I'll get Kushner to donate it. I'll speak to his nephew, Frank. Lou's too cheap, but Frank'll do it. I'll tell him it's for the Y, but I won't tell him who's gonna be eating it."

"Are you sure you want to do this?" I asked. "Eleanore said the prepared fish will be fine. They really won't know the difference."

"*I'll* know the difference!" she said. And that was that.

My mother called Eleanore a few days later to remind her that she was going to be making the gefilte fish for the seder. She also suggested that she would bring over from the bakery some honey cakes and macaroon cookies, the chocolate ones, because teenagers would only eat macaroons if they were covered in chocolate. Eleanore reminded her that while the seder would be starting at seven o'clock, she should plan on being there about 5:30, as they would need plenty of time to set everything up.

"Do they know about the shank bones and the *charoses*?" my mother asked.

Eleanore assured her that Rabbi Stein from Young Israel had been working with the Y's cook, Mrs. MacElroy, and that he had filled her in on the entire seder meal.

"How can an Irish woman cook Jewish food?" my mother asked.

Eleanore carefully explained to her that Phyllis MacElroy was not Irish, but a Negro woman who had cooked for Jewish families for many years. Then she told her that Mrs. MacElroy had actually made a point of telling her how happy she was that a Jewish grandmother was making the gefilte fish. That seemed to assuage my mother's doubts, at least temporarily.

On the afternoon of the event, I left work early, picked up my mother-in-law who was going to baby-sit, dropped her off at my apartment, and then drove over to my father's bakery. I loaded the car with several large boxes of cakes and cookies. It looked to me as if there was enough for a hundred and seventy kids, not just the seventy who were expected at the seder. My father said that my mother had been at the bakery earlier to supervise the packing. "Be careful," he warned me. "She's a real hurricane today!"

When I arrived at my parents' apartment, my mother was already waiting with her coat on. She was neatly groomed, but her ostentatious diamond earring studs had been replaced by simple ceramic earrings. So far so good, I thought.

"Those," she said, pointing to three large foil-wrapped pans of gefilte fish sitting on the kitchen table. "If you can handle two, I'll carry one."

As we made our way through the door, she looked at me anxiously. "You have all the cakes in the car?"

"Of course, I do. Eleanore reminded me after you called her this afternoon, even before you called to remind me," I muttered.

"Don't be snotty. I just want everything to go well. It's important that everything is perfect."

I pulled up in front of the Y and ran inside to see if I could get some help in unloading our Jewish culinary treasures. I returned a few minutes later with three Black kids, one of whom was wearing a blue team jacket with white lettering that spelled out "YOUNG MEN'S & YOUNG WOMEN'S HEBREW ASSOCIATION" across the back. My mother squinted as she read the words. It was hard to tell what she was thinking.

The seder was going to be held in the Y's basement dining room. It was decorated with blue and white balloons, and red, white and blue crepe paper—in honor, I guessed, of Israel and the United States of America. There were seven round tables, each with seating for ten, and one long table at the front of the room, close to the kitchen, which I later learned was for Harry Katz, the rabbi and the minister, several officials from the Federation of Jewish Philanthropies and the Boys Clubs of America and, of course, Eleanore.

The seder, apparently, would double as a sort of "changing of the guard" event; clearly my mother's gefilte fish was going to be a symbol of the old order. I could see that she sensed its importance. A small smile on her face told me she was confident of success.

"Where's this MacElroy woman?" she asked as soon as she saw Eleanore.

"Oh, I'll go get her," said Harry, who was standing at Eleanore's side. "She's very anxious to meet you."

"I'm right here," said a small, dark-complexioned Negro woman, emerging from behind a huge basket of flowers at the head table. She looked to be about sixty years old. "You must be Eleanore's mother-in-law. I have to tell you, Mrs. Korman, I just tasted your gefilte fish—and it was heaven!"

My mother beamed. "Well, thank you, Mrs. MacElroy."

"Oh, dear, it's Phyllis—or Phyll, to my friends."

"And I'm Lilly," my mother said.

"Lil and Phyll," Harry noted. "Sounds like a vaudeville team."

Everyone laughed except my mother, who was still a bit uncertain about this Mrs. MacElroy.

The rituals of the seder went off with the precision of a marching band at a championship football game. One of the teenagers, the one with the team jacket, was assigned the role of the leader. Promptly at seven o'clock, he stood and raised his glass of Welch's Grape Juice and recited the Hebrew prayer: *"Bo-ruch a-toh a-do-noy, el-o-hay-noo me-lech ha-a-lom, bor-ray pree ha-go-fen."* And then he spoke in English: "Blessed art thou, O Lord our God, King of the Universe, who created the fruit of the vine."

All of the adults beamed, and most of the teenagers giggled. In rapid succession, the various rituals of the seder went forward. The traditional "Four Questions" were asked by the youngest present, a tiny Hispanic girl who spoke with the confidence of a valedictorian at Harvard; the leader called on various members of the group to read portions of the *Haggadah,* which told the story of the Israelites' flight from slavery under the Egyptian Pharaohs; and everyone joined in the ritual recitation of the "Plagues," dipping their pinkies into their glasses of grape juice in order to diminish the amount of "wine" and—symbolically—the suffering of their enemies.

From a seat at one of the back tables, I looked across the room at Eleanore, who was sitting at the head table next to the Baptist minister. She seemed to be enjoying herself, and I saw by her gestures that she was busily explaining in great detail to the minister and the representatives from the Boys Clubs exactly how one ate the *moror* and the *charoses,* two of the symbolic foods which preceded the actual dinner. I could almost read her lips as she explained that the *moror,* the potent horseradish served on a piece of matzo, represented the bitterness of slavery, and the *charoses,* a combination of chopped apples and nuts and rich grape wine, the sweetness of God's redemption.

I spotted my mother going from table to table with Mrs. MacElroy. I had no idea what they were saying to one another or to the kids. But it could not have been easy explaining everything to seventy teenagers who, until that moment, hadn't known a matzo from a burnt shank bone—if that, indeed, was what the two were talking about. I imagined my mother describing the flat cracker that was the matzo to the teenagers as a symbol of the haste in which the Israelites had fled Egypt.

Just before the meal was served, the rabbi stood up and, in the lofty tones that rabbis and ministers have developed over the centuries, reminded the kids that while he hoped they would have a good time, it was important for them to remember that Passover was about freedom from slavery, and that both the Jews and the Negroes had once been slaves.

"What about us?" whispered a Puerto Rican kid who was sitting at my table. His friends snickered.

There was a scattering of applause as the rabbi sat down.

"Does this mean we get to eat now?" another kid at my table asked.

"Unless you want more speeches," his friend joked.

Indeed, it was time for the meal to begin. The food was served by the Y's staff and by members of the Young Adult Chorus, who were scheduled to entertain the group once the meal was over.

Everything was served on plates decorated with the Star of David. The first course was my mother's gefilte fish. Each plate contained one patty of fish and a dab of beet-flavored horseradish. Predictably, most of the kids turned up their noses at the horseradish.

"Isn't there something else we can put on the fish?" one kid shouted. Hearing this, Mrs. MacElroy dashed into the kitchen and brought out several bottles of ketchup. The kids began making matzo sandwiches consisting of gefilte fish and ketchup.

"This is great," one of my tablemates said. "It's even better than the Busy Bee hamburgers."

Ketchup on gefilte fish might have been unconventional, but it worked.

I looked over toward my mother. She was totally expressionless.

The rest of the meal went pretty much as expected. The chicken soup with matzo balls was a big hit, and the roasted chickens, mashed potatoes and asparagus were consumed with almost manic energy. The teens at my table barely looked up from their plates from one mouthful to the next. The only things that remained to be served were the honey cake and the chocolate-covered macaroons, but they were scheduled after the entertainment, which was about to begin.

The Y's Young Adult Chorus, eight woman and four men, still wearing their waiters' aprons, gathered in front of the long table. The lights in the hall were dimmed, and all conversation stopped. After a few tentative sounds from a pitch pipe, the chorus erupted, singing with enormous gusto—and most appropriately—the great Negro spiritual, "Let My People Go." After this, they managed a spirited version of the Israeli national anthem, "*Hatikvah*." As an encore, and for no apparent reason except that it must have been part of their repertoire, they sang, "You Gotta Have Heart," the Washington Senators' fight song from the then-current Broadway hit, *Damn Yankees*.

Midway through the latter, some kids at a table near where I was sitting began a small food war, hurling pieces of matzo at one another. It had been a long evening. But, miraculously, out came the honey cakes and the macaroons, along with Dr. Pepper and 7-Up. The kids went back into their eating mode and the war ended.

While the massive cleanup was underway, the people at the head table were busy congratulating each other and anyone else who happened by. The Baptist minister put his arm around my mother. "Your daughter-in-law has told me," he intoned in his rich, pulpit-trained bass voice, "that while Mrs. MacElroy was responsible for that mar-velous matzo ball soup and those splendid roasted chickens, that the ge-fil-tah fish was your doing. I want to tell you, Lil—I hope you are not offended if I call you Lil?—that the fish was sublime. It was *the* best ge-fil-tah fish I have ever eaten, and believe me, I have eaten ge-fil-tah fish many times." He beamed.

My mother beamed back. "I didn't know . . . " she paused for just a beat, "that . . . er . . . Negroes knew about gefilte fish."

"Indeed, some of us do. When I was growing up, my mother—may she rest in peace—worked as a cleaning woman and cook for a Jewish family on West End Avenue. Ge-fil-tah fish was a Friday night staple. That fine lady taught my mother how to make it. Excellent, but not as good as yours, I might add."

My mother could not have been happier. "Wasn't that sweet of the reverend to single out my gefilte fish?" she gushed after he'd stepped away.

"Hey, it was well-deserved," Mrs. MacElroy said. "Chicken soup with dumplings and roast chickens are one thing, but gefilte fish—now that's really something!"

"Especially when you pour ketchup on top," I pointed out wickedly.

"Actually, Phyll saved the day," my mother added. "I think the fish would have bombed without the ketchup."

The two women walked off together to continue their conversation. I marveled at how similar they appeared: two small creatures, each a bit on the chunky side, with soft, curly heads of gray hair. The length of their dresses matched exactly, and their shoes looked as if they had been bought at a two-for-one sale.

My mother and Phyll became friends. Once a week or so, they would escape from their respective chores at the family bakery and the Boys Club kitchen. They went on shopping sprees at Macy's, had lunch in the Automat, went to Radio City Music Hall; in the summer, they took a train out to Long Beach and spent a day in the sun.

When Phyll's granddaughter graduated from high school, my mother was invited to the ceremony and to the party afterwards.

They were Lil and Phyll.

A few years later, Phyllis MacElroy suffered a stroke. My mother received a distraught telephone call from Phyll's granddaughter, who said that Phyll was in serious condition at Bronx-Lebanon Hospital. My mother called me immediately and asked if I would drive her there the next day.

Phyll was in a semi-private room that had been arranged for her by the Boys Club. She seemed tinier than I remembered, just a small, dark face surrounded by white pillows and sheets.

My mother took her friend's bony brown hand and held it. "Phyll, it's me, Lil." Even if Mrs. MacElroy could not at that moment process the meaning of the words, the melody of their sound seemed to convey the message to her.

Phyll never recovered. I drove my mother to the funeral service at Bethany Baptist where the Reverend talked about Phyll's gentleness and good works. He never mentioned her chickens or her matzo ball soup, but I imagined he was tasting them throughout his eulogy.

Many years went by, and when my mother grew frail, she moved into the Hebrew Home for the Aged in Riverdale. The year was 1986. A number of her fellow residents were African-Americans, as were most of the staff. I would visit her there every week, and she would ramble on about the people in the home. She carefully referred to them as Blacks or Negroes. She never once said *schwarzer*.

Epilogue

Business in my father's bakery dwindled because there was little demand for rye breads and challahs, babkas and streusel cakes from the African-American and Latino families who had moved into the neighborhood. Still, the bakery survived until 1962 when my father retired.

My parents moved to Florida where they stayed until my father grew bored playing pinochle and going to Hialeah to bet on the horses. Within a year, they were back in their beloved Bronx and had opened a new bakery near Lydig Avenue and White Plains Road, in one of the borough's few remaining Jewish neighborhoods. They worked there until various illnesses made it impossible for my father to continue. He sold the bakery and retired a second time, spending most of his days going to the track and playing pinochle at night in his old club in Yorkville.

He was happy because he could work weekends as a bread baker for his son-in-law, my sister's husband, who had a bakery on 167th Street near Jerome Avenue. One early morning, after a full night of pinochle in Yorkville, he collapsed at the worktable with a half-shaped Kaiser roll in his hand. He was dead two days later. It could be said that he died with his apron on.